PREACHING AS THEOLOGY &ART

Elizabeth Achtemeier

Abingdon Press

Nashville

Preaching as Theology and Art

Copyright © 1984 by Abingdon Press

All rights reserved.
No part of this book may be reproduced in any manner
whatsoever without written permission of the publisher
except brief quotations embodied in critical articles or
reviews. For information address Abingdon Press,
Nashville, Tennessee.

Library of Congress Cataloging in Publication Data

ACHTEMEIER, ELIZABETH RICE, 1926-
    Preaching as theology and art.
    Includes bibliographical references.
    1. Preaching. 2. Sermons, American. 3. Medita-
tions. I. Title.
BV4211.2.A28   1984   251   83-11839
            ISBN 0-687-33828-X

Selections on pages 95, 97 are from "Electric Chimes or Rams' Horns" by
Amos N. Wilder. Copyright 1971 by the Christian Century Foundation.
Reprinted by permission from the January 27, 1971 issue of *The Christian
Century.* Lines from "The Hollow Men" in *Collected Poems 1909-1962* by T. S.
Eliot are on page 67, copyright 1936 by Harcourt Brace Jovanovich, Inc.;
copyright © 1963, 1964 by T. S. Eliot. Reprinted by permission of Harcourt,
Brace, Jovanovich and Faber & Faber Ltd. Selections on pages 64-65 are
from *The Lives of a Cell* by Lewis Thomas. Copyright © 1971 by the
Massachusetts Medical Society. Originally published in *The New England
Journal of Medicine.* Reprinted by permission of Viking Penguin, Inc.
Selections on pages 62-62 are from *Pilgrim at Tinker Creek* by Annie Dillard,
copyright 1974 by Harper & Row. Lines on page 73 are from *A Sleep of
Prisoners* by Christopher Fry, copyright 1951 by Oxford University Press.
Lines from *God's Trombones* by James Weldon Johnson are on page 62.
Copyright © 1927 by The Viking Press. Copyright renewed 1955 by Grace
Nail Johnson. Reprinted by permision of Viking Penguin, Inc.

Scripture quotations unless otherwise noted are from the Revised Standard
Version of the Bible, copyrighted 1946, 1952, © 1971, 1973 by the Division
of Christian Education of the National Council of the Churches of Christ in
the U.S.A., and are used by permission. Quotations noted KJV are from
the King James Version of the Bible.

MANUFACTURED BY THE PARTHENON PRESS AT
NASHVILLE, TENNESSEE, UNITED STATES OF AMERICA

To the faculty and administration
of Union Theological Seminary in Richmond, Virginia,
in gratitude
for their commitment to the church

CONTENTS

PREFACE...7

I. PREACHING AS THEOLOGY...................... 9

A. Preaching Judgment and Forgiveness................... 20
   Sample Meditations:
     GOD THE JUDGE?.....................................22
       Scripture: John 12:27-33
                  Isaiah 28:9-13, 16-17, 19-22
     TIT FOR TAT?...25
       Scripture: Romans 5:8-9
                  Jonah 3-4
     THE PURPOSE OF FORGIVENESS.....................28
       Scripture: John 15:9-11
                  Psalm 130
                  Romans 6:1-4, 12-12

B. Preaching about Poor and Rich,
   Oppressed and Oppressors............................. 30
   Sample Meditations:
     THE YELLOW BICYCLE.................................. 32
       Scripture: Matthew 5:23-24
                  Deuteronomy 15:7-11

ON ROMANTICIZING THE POOR AND
    OPPRESSED..35
    Scripture: Jeremiah 5:1-6

C. Preaching about God's Work in Nature................ 38
    Sample Meditation: *SEASONS' MEANING*............ 39
    Scripture: Genesis 6:5-8; 8:20-22

D. Preaching the Kingdom of God........................... 41
    Sample Meditation: *THE KINGDOM COME*.......... 43
    Scripture: 2 Corinthians 6:2
           Isaiah 61:1-3
           Luke 4:14-21

E. Preaching One Holy Catholic Church................... 46
    Sample Meditation: *THE RICHES OF*
    THE CHURCH.. 47
    Scripture: Ephesians 3:1-19

II. PREACHING AS THEOLOGY
    AND ART..51

A. Doxology...59
    Sample Sermon: *GOD THE MUSIC LOVER*...........62
    Scripture: Psalm 148
           Colossians 1:9-20

B. Preaching for Advent/Christmas.......................... 70
    Sample Sermon: *OF REPENTANCE*
    AND CAPTIVITY..72
    Scripture: Luke 3:1-18

C. Preaching for Epiphany..................................... 81
    Sample Sermon: *ON LIVING IN REALITY*.............84
    Scripture: Exodus 33:12-18
           John 14:1-11

D. Preaching for Epiphany (continued)..................... 91
    Sample Sermon: *OUR ORDINARY WORSHIP*........93
    Scripture: Exodus 19:10-19
           Hebrews 12:18-29

E. Preaching for Lent..102
   Sample Sermon: *THE JOURNEY—THE CHOICE*... 106
     Scripture: Deuteronomy 30:15-20
          Matthew 7:13-29

F. Preaching for Eastertide....................................113
   Sample Sermon: *DEALING WITH THE
   FINAL FOE*..116
     Scripture: Luke 24:1-11
          1 Corinthians 15:17-28

G. Preaching for Pentecost....................................122
   Sample Sermon: *THE EASY YOKE*....................124
     Scripture: Jeremiah 2:20-28
          Matthew 11:28-30

H. Preaching for Pentecost (continued)....................133
   Sample Sermon: *THE WRESTLING*....................135
     Scripture: Genesis 32:13-32
          2 Corinthians 4:5-12

NOTES..143

PREFACE

This book was originally suggested by readers of my 1980 volume, *Creative Preaching*, who asked that the full text of some of the sermons excerpted in that volume be printed. This book now fulfills that request.

Since the publication of *Creative Preaching*, however, continued experience and reflection as a teacher of homiletics have led me to see that preachers must be thoroughly trained, not only in Bible but also in Christian theology. Apart from the latter discipline, preachers do not understand the Bible as Scripture. They have a hard time developing a sermon, sometimes neglecting to proclaim the gospel or even lapsing into heresy. This volume addresses those concerns.

At the same time, I believe that the proclamation of the gospel of Jesus Christ demands the best rhetorical skill that we preachers can bring to it. *Creative Preaching* discussed at length the development of such skill. I hope that the meditations, sermons, and the introductions to them in this subsequent volume will illustrate and supplement what was said in that earlier book.

Elizabeth Achtemeier
Union Theological Seminary
Richmond, Virginia

7

Part One

PREACHING AS THEOLOGY

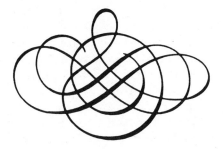

Christian preaching is, above all else, the proclamation of the Word of God—the interpretation of a biblical text for a listening congregation—and thereby the release of the powerful word of that text into the hearts and minds and lives of the gathered people, to work its judgment and salvation, its cleansing and mercy, its motivation to repentance and praise and service among those opened to receive its action.

Books and teachers dealing with homiletics have therefore largely concentrated their attention in the past on the necessity of preaching from the Bible. They have rightly inveighed against sermons that do nothing more than dispense psychological and mental health principles, that impose the preacher's opinions on the Scripture, or that ignore the actions of God through the Scriptures and exhort the people to rise to new moral levels on their own.

Lately, in the literature of homiletics, attention to the biblical text has been fostered by emphasizing the narrative quality of the Bible and by urging preachers to "tell the story" and to let their people identify with it, or with some character in it.[1] Scholars have also singled out the various forms or genres of literature in the Bible, and preachers have been urged to discover how these forms involved their original hearers and to duplicate that involvement among

9

their own listeners by the way they use the various textual forms in their sermons.[2] All of this has been helpful to the task of preaching.

Little specific attention has been given, however, to the preacher as theologian. Perhaps only among the more evangelistic and fundamentalist groups has there been emphasis on the fact that every sermon must find its context within a body of traditional Christian doctrine. And while evangelistic and fundamentalistic preachers have some-times ignored the specificity of their texts in favor of the more general doctrine, nevertheless they have preserved the necessary relation of Bible and tradition.[3]

The Christian faith carries with it a specific, traditional content, which has been formulated across the centuries by the church on the basis of the biblical witness. As is well-known, C. H. Dodd found within the New Testament itself a central kerygma or proclamation characteristic of the early church, which had approximately the following outline:

1. The age of fulfillment, or the coming of the kingdom of God, is at hand.
2. This coming has taken place through the ministry, death, and resurrection of Jesus.
3. By virtue of the resurrection, Jesus is exalted at the right hand of God as the messianic head of the new Israel.
4. The Holy Spirit in the church is the sign of Christ's present power and glory.
5. The messianic age will shortly reach its consummation in the second coming of Christ.
6. Forgiveness, the Holy Spirit, and salvation come with repentance.[4]

Such was the core content of Christian preaching, according to Dodd, in the first and second century New Testament materials.

As the church grew and spread in the Roman Empire, instructing new converts and guarding against heresy, it became necessary to define the relation of the Father, Son, and Holy Spirit in the Nicean Creed of the fourth century, and to confess the divine and human natures of Jesus Christ, "unconfused and undivided," in the Chalcedonian

10

formula of the fifth century. Within the Western Church, by the eighth or ninth century, the Apostles' Creed became the dominant expression of Christian belief, a status that it still holds today.

In short, the Christian preacher stands within a theological tradition, which he or she cannot ignore and still claim to be Christian. There is a basic Christian understanding of who Jesus Christ is; of what his relation to the Father and the Spirit is; of what has taken place in the sacred, biblical history; of what the goal of human history will be; and of how the Christian is incorporated into the purposes of God. The church has formulated these basic Christian understandings—in other words, its theology—in a dialogue with the world and on the foundation of the Scriptures' witness. While some preachers may formulate other understandings of the Christian faith, whether or not those formulations are specifically Christian depends on whether or not they are consonant with the church's core theology.

The Christian preacher is not a lone voice, crying in a wilderness of unbelief, proclaiming a message never heard before on earth. He or she is a "steward of the mysteries of God," to use Paul's phrase, a recipient of a biblical and theological tradition handed down across twenty centuries of Christian faith and practice. And as the apostle writes, "It is required of stewards that they be found trustworthy" (I Corinthians 4:2)—that is, that they hear the Christian proclamation that has gone before them, that they preserve it in relation to their own time and place, that they announce its message for their own society's unique situation, and that they pass it on unspoiled and undistorted by the fads and fancies of current sin and opinion.

This does not mean that the preacher is an antiquarian, interested only in the thought of the past. Nor does it mean that the preacher is a rigid dogmatist, refusing constantly to reformulate Christian theology in the language of his or her own time. Traditional Christian understandings must be continually rethought and rewritten, allowing the gospel to speak afresh to each new generation and society; hence the church has an ongoing history of creedal formulation and reformulation. But what these statements do recognize is that there is a "given" to Christian theology—a core belief, grounded in a biblical history that has taken place, apart from which any theological formulation ceases to be Christian. I have characterized that core belief as the theology summed up in the Nicene and Apostles' Creeds and in the Chalcedonian formulation, because those theological summaries are most universally recognized in the church as valid expressions of the thought of traditional Christianity.

In order to claim that he or she stands in the long line of that great "cloud of witnesses" who have passed down the Christian tradition from generation to generation, the preacher therefore has to absorb basic Christian theology into his or her own personal faith and experience, until it becomes almost automatically present. That Christian theology then forms the context, checks the content, and illumines the exposition of every sermon preached.

Contrary to the impression given in some books on homiletics, it is not enough for a Christian preacher to exegete and expound a single biblical pericope in a sermon. The single passage of Scripture is contained within a canon that interprets the individual pericope: "Scripture interprets Scripture." And the preacher has always to ask if his or her interpretation of the single pericope accords with the witness of Scripture as a whole. But that witness of Scripture is summarized for us in the theological tradition of the church. The preacher can therefore ask theological questions about his or her sermon:

> Is God glorified in the sermon as "the Father Almighty, Maker of heaven and earth," or has he perhaps been identified with someone or something in his creation? Indeed, in this time, is there any understanding of his unique Fatherhood at all?
>
> Is the sermon Trinitarian, or has it emphasized one Person of the Trinity to the exclusion of the other two, as if somehow God no longer has anything to do with Jesus or with the Spirit?

Does the proclamation reflect the true humanity and true godhead of Jesus Christ, or has he been turned into a merely human moral example or into a simply superhuman God, thus denying the Incarnation?

Does the sermon confess the Holy Spirit as the Creator and Sustainer of the church, or has the Body of Christ been characterized as a human organization, existing only by its own strength and self-inspired conviction?

Do God's immediate work in his world and the consummation of his purpose form the hope that is held out to the congregation, or has the rule of God been replaced by the rule of human beings?

For every sermon, the theological tradition of the church, rooted in the biblical witness, lurks in the back of the preacher's mind as the judge of the sermon's theology. By thus being a *church theologian*, the preacher often preaches a much more truly biblical sermon than do those homileticians who concentrate on a single biblical text but who ignore the text's context in the total Scriptural witness, which is distilled, in turn, in the church's theology.

Certainly the Christian pulpit is often suffering these days from non-biblical preaching. Worst of all, it is sometimes suffering from heretical preaching. For example, a California clergyman recently said to me, "I believe that we are all incarnations of God." That clergyman and others like him are preaching non-biblical sermons, not only because they do not know what the Bible says and how to study it, but also because they do not understand the most basic theology of the Christian church. The Christian preacher must be biblical scholar *and* church theologian, and it is perhaps the latter role that has not been emphasized enough in our day.

Because many preachers have not been adequately trained in Christian theology, they often have a difficult time developing the final, crucial points of their sermons. I have found in teaching homiletics over the years that even the weakest students can usually write two sections of a sermon. They can more or less illumine the historical situation of Israel or of the New Testament church in the biblical text for the day, and above all else, they can illumine the present sinful situation of their own society. At great length and in vivid detail and illustration, they can illumine it! Sometimes they even can compare or contrast the latter with the situation in the biblical text. But then the students get stuck, because they have reached the point in the sermon where they have to bring the details of the text to bear on our sinful society, and that involves expertise not only in biblical exposition but also in Christian theology. If the text proclaims the judgment of God, they have to spell out how and where God is at work in judgment in our world. If forgiveness is announced, they have to know something about how forgiveness is mediated to the believer, and what faith means, and how the grace of God is appropriated by the individual in the Body of Christ. If the text deals with the atoning work of Jesus Christ, they have to be able to handle the doctrine of atonement and then apply it to their congregation in vivid and meaningful and clear language. In short, they have to have thought through the whole system of Christian theology, and made it an integral part of their own thought and speech and action.

It is not difficult to analyze and describe what is wrong with our society; even a twelve-year-old child can do that. Illustrations of our sickness-unto-death leap out from every headline and fill every TV screen. And many preachers love to dwell on just how sinfully sick we are. But to paraphrase Jeremiah's language (8:22), in the the words of the Negro spiritual, "There is a balm in Gilead to heal the sin-sick soul." Healing has come. The good news has been announced. God has reconciled the world to himself in Jesus Christ, and that saving action has altered the course of human history and the context and meaning of every human life. The Christian preacher has been called, therefore, to announce the good news and to spell out its implications and to trace its effects in ordinary day-by-day living. But only the Christian preacher solidly grounded in church theology can begin to fulfill that task.

For this reason, many preachers prostitute their calling.

They have not thought through the whole system of Christian theology, and so they cannot bring it to bear on common, ordinary human life. They take refuge in empty moralisms, admonishing their congregations, in so many words, to "get out there and do good" or "just try to have more faith." Or they abandon the biblical message altogether and become purveyors of mental health, and we get sermons on "How to Live with Yourself" or "Five Ways to Overcome Anxiety" in the pulpit's version of *Reader's Digest* religion. Or perhaps worst of all, they become the prophets of doom and gloom: they describe in lurid details what is wrong with American society; they then leave their congregations wallowing in guilt, or they end their sermons with vague and generalized assurances that nevertheless their parishioners have been saved and have had new meaning given to their lives. But what does it mean "to be saved" as we pursue our common, everyday rounds of work? Or what *is* the new meaning given by Jesus Christ to my ordinary life as a housewife and a mother? It takes solid, theological thought to answer those questions.

It also takes solid, theological training to preach with rational consistency, so that the sum of all one's proclamation forms an integrated whole. The ordinary minister develops and delivers at least fifty sermons a year. In that process, he or she deals with many different biblical texts, each having its own particular theological nuances and views. This variety of theologies found in the Scriptures is not to be overlooked or homogenized, nor is each individual text to be harmonized with every other. Precisely by uncovering the unique theology of each of the four gospels, for example, does the expositor get at what Mark and Matthew and Luke and John were saying about Jesus. Sermons developed out of a harmonization of the four gospels really do not proclaim the evangelists' unique testimonies, as the three-year ecumenical lectionary has tried to stress by concentrating on one synoptic gospel per year.

Nevertheless, the varying theologies found in both the New Testament and the Old stand in one over-arching history of creation-fall-judgment-redemption, with major motifs, such as election and covenant, running through that history from beginning to end. Despite all the Bible's diversity, and despite the demurrers of some recent scholarship, there is a basic *Heilsgeschichte*, finally summed up and fulfilled in Jesus Christ, into which every theology found in the Bible fits.[5] This sacred history has been summarized in the church's major creedal formulations, and the primary saving events, told in the *Heilsgeschichte*, have been used to form the central core of Christian theology out of which all else is developed. If the preacher is rooted and grounded in that church theology, he or she is much less likely to contradict himself or herself over the span of a year's or several years' preaching. He or she is thus much less likely to confuse and mystify the congregation. There is a consistency lent to the preacher's message of judgment or sin or election or redemption. God does not suddenly change character in the jump from the Old Testament to New. His purposes and his demands for human life and history remain the same. His workings move steadily toward the goal of the kingdom of God on earth. And his sovereign grace shines through the testimony of every text.

At the same time, the preacher who has made the church's theology the warp and woof of his or her own thought and experience is given the resources to preach with great variety. In one sense, we preachers announce the same message over and over again, year in and year out—the message of God's love for humankind in creation and his redemption of us, because of that love, in Jesus Christ our Lord. If we use the lectionary, we even have to return to the same biblical texts over and over again, and we sometimes have the feeling that there is nothing new to say, or at least no new way to tell "the old, old story." But we have the resources of two thousand years of church theology to draw on, and Luther and Calvin, Irenaeus and Chrysostom, Niebuhr and Barth, and all the other fathers of the church can help us find new expressions of a gospel that they too believed and preached. In what a glorious company we stand! Yet, we are prevented from lapsing into heresy—and even the fathers were sometimes wrong when measured by the biblical authority!—just as we are enabled to eschew the merely novel, because we are taught and guided by the central affirmations of the Christian faith. The center is firm, the core theology is solid. We can then move out from that center, in conversation with every area and opinion of modern life, to bring the gospel to bear upon them.

Finally, the preacher who has made the church's theology his or her own possession is able from the pulpit to educate the congregation in the Christian faith. In my own Reformed tradition, the minister is appropriately known as a "teaching elder," and under that rubric, he or she has two very important tasks. First of all, as the congregation's church theologian, the minister has the task of educating the congregation in the central beliefs of Christianity. This is not a task that is performed only in confirmation class or in the church school. For far too long we have turned the responsibility for Christian education over to the Sunday school, with mixed results. Long before there was a Sunday school, faithful clergy taught their congregations Christian theology in their Sunday sermons, and traditional Christian theology has been preserved in the church. One new generation after another of educated Christians has been raised up, because some preachers have been trustworthy stewards and teachers of the theological tradition handed down to them.

On this score, probably one of the most disastrous devices ever invented by Christian educators and preachers has been the practice of having a children's "sermon" or "moment" in the Sunday worship service *and then dismissing the children* to a classroom for play or instruction on their level. Contrary to some modern Christian educational theory, children absorb the Christian faith by hearing it read and sung and preached and celebrated in the liturgy Sunday after Sunday, year after year. Phrases from its Scriptures become as familiar as mother and father. The praises and laments of its prayers become the model of how

17

to pray. The teaching of its doctrines, set forth vividly in sermons, becomes the guide and content of belief and ethical practice. To be sure, children who participate in the Sunday morning service have to be trained in reverent behavior, but that too is part of their Christian education, and the preacher—in that Sunday service—is fully as responsible for Christian education as are Sunday school and parents.

This does not mean, of course, that the Sunday sermon is to be turned into a theological lecture. Abstract theological discussion is neither very interesting nor understandable to the average adult, much less to children—although it is amazing how eager the average congregation is to *know* what Christianity teaches. But the preacher teaches Christian theology in his or her sermon by dealing with the central affirmations of the Christian faith, as prompted by the biblical text for the day, and by spelling out the implications of those affirmations for the congregation's day-by-day life. This is where a congregation learns what the Christian faith means for its living—from its preacher, who illumines that meaning by presenting the dialogue of the biblical faith with the world of the parishioner.

Second, as the congregation's church theologian, the preacher has the task of enabling his or her people to mature in their faith and practice. The Christian life is not a static state of being. It is a growth up into "the measure of the stature of the fullness of Christ," a growth in holiness and understanding, a growth in obedience and service, in short, a growth in sanctification. The Bible, therefore, always characterizes the people of God as underway, as moving toward a goal, as "forgetting what lies behind and straining forward to what lies ahead" (Philippians 3:13).

Instead, far too many preachers leave their people in the same place, content with the understanding and commitment that the people had before the minister ever took the church. In the words of Hebrews, the preacher teaches his or her people "the first principles of God's word," the "elementary doctrines of Christ," over and over and over again. The congregation is kept on "milk," and never fed "solid food," and therefore they never grow up to be adults

18

in the faith. And usually the reason for that is that the minister is not a mature theologian, who can take the central affirmations of the biblical, Christian witness and spell out their implications for our time and life.

The practice of church theology is a matter of receiving a traditional, biblical body of Christian understanding—of absorbing that basic theology into one's own bones until it becomes automatically the context and guide of one's own thought and practice, then carrying on a constant dialogue with and critique of one's own society and culture in the light of that Christian understanding. As that dialogue and critique go on—every day—the preacher constantly finds new ways of expressing Christian theology, new insights into its meaning, new growth in his or her own personal apprehension and practice of the faith. Yet the core of that understanding remains firm, and its central affirmations do not change: the preacher takes his or her stand solidly in the midst of that great "cloud of witnesses" who across the centuries have confessed that Jesus Christ is Lord.

The eight brief meditations that follow are intended to illustrate this practice of church theology. All of them were preached before seminary students in Watts Chapel of Union Theological Seminary in Richmond, Virginia, during the fifteen minute chapel service that takes place there four mornings a week. All of them grew out of a biblical text or texts, although because of the brevity of the service, some of the texts were used as calls to worship or responsive readings, as indicated. All of the meditations can be expanded into full-length sermons. All of them deal with traditional, biblical Christian theology. And all of them use that theology to converse with or to critique contemporary American culture. In a preface to each, I have discussed some of the theological questions involved and the situations in our culture toward which the meditation is directed. By presenting these brief homilies in this manner, I hope that readers will be stimulated anew to that theological reflection, based on the Bible and Christian tradition, which should be so much a part of Christian preaching.

A. Preaching Judgment and Forgiveness

Central to the Christian gospel is the glad proclamation that we are forgiven our sin against God through his act of mercy in the death and resurrection of his Son Jesus Christ. That message is probably announced more frequently from Christian pulpits than is any other portion of the gospel—although, contrary to the theology of Paul (cf. I Corinthians 15:17), most preachers connect forgiveness with the cross alone, apart from the resurrection.

Because in our time the forgiveness of God has been broadcast so frequently and widely in the land, it has unfortunately become almost a truism, taken for granted by religious people. "Of course God forgives," said George Bernard Shaw, "that's his business." God's costly act of mercy has become separated from its moorings in the historical sacrifice and victory of Christ and turned into an automatic gesture of benevolence on the part of a kindly old deity. The populace assumes a loving Father who forgives, and presumes he takes no offense at them, providing they are doing the best they can.

Such attitudes toward the forgiveness of God witness to a widespread ignorance of the righteous character of God and of the depth of human sinfulness, eliminating from our preaching and our people's lives any concern with the judgment of God upon them, whether that judgment be present or future. God does not judge in modern America; he forgives. Therefore, while most ministers announce the mercy of the Lord, few frame any scriptural sermons about his judgments, despite the fact that the figure of God as judge is prominent throughout the Bible. A final judgment seems anachronistic to modern preachers, and they have not thought much about some sort of present judgment. Indeed, many would be hard-pressed to point to any evidence of God's judging actions within our everyday lives.

The result is that the Christian gospel has largely lost its urgency for our people, and the evangelistic and missionary enterprises of the mainline churches have been undercut.

During a speech at an evangelism conference three years ago, I made the statement, "The Christian gospel is a matter of life or death." A religious book editor found that a "radical assertion" and inquired whether or not I would like to write a book about it! In a culture that assumes God forgives and bestows blessings and eternal life upon us, no matter what we do or believe, there is no urgency about calling persons to faith in Jesus Christ. Nor is there an urgency about making Christian disciples of all nations. Salvation has become a human right, bestowed on all indiscriminately, by a God who demands nothing and gives all.

To be sure, there are many faithful and believing persons within our congregations who know that they daily stand under the covenant demands of God, and who confess that apart from God's mercy toward them in the death and resurrection of his Son, they would have no fellowship with God, no righteousness of their own, no hope of life or good. But even among such faithful Christians, the implications of God's forgiveness must be spelled out, lest they turn forgiveness into a reward for repentance or a sanction for cheap grace—not only for themselves, but for others toward whom they wish to act in a Christian manner.

Such distortions in our understandings of God's judgment and mercy also have far-reaching consequences for our society. I believe it true to say that the life-style of the U.S. during the last two decades, with its moral lassitude and easy acceptance of "anything goes," has been deeply influenced by a perversion of the Christian doctrine of forgiveness. Therefore the church must re-examine its preaching of that doctrine if it wishes to restore any sense of Christian morality in our time. As is so often the case, the mote may not be in the others' eyes, but in our own.

The three meditations that follow attempt to set forth some biblical understandings of forgiveness and of God's judgment. They were intended to stimulate further thought about these theological problems on the part of the clergy and the candidates for the ministry to whom they were addressed.

Sample Meditation:

GOD THE JUDGE?

Scripture: John 12:27-33 (Call to Worship)
Isaiah 28:9-13, 16-17, 19-22

We have difficulty with the judgments of God in the Old Testament. I have never taught a course in Old Testament in which someone has not objected to, or at least questioned, the Old Testament's portrayal of God as a God of wrath and judgment. And when the same God is pointed to in the New Testament's witness, this has usually occasioned a look of uneasiness, if not downright disbelief, on the questioner's face. The God and Father of our Lord Jesus Christ is not, to our minds, a judge, and of course there are several reasons why that is so.

On the superficial surface of our lives, we are not sure, first of all, that we deserve any judgment. After all, we are faithful church people, dedicated Christians, who are sincerely doing the very best we can. And when Genesis 3 portrays God's radical judgment against the whole of his creation, or when God looks at human beings at the beginning of the flood story and mourns, "I am sorry that I have made them," we are quite sure that is spoken about the other guys—about the really bad sinners in our world—and not about us. How could God actually be sorry that he has made you and me? A tyrant like Khomeini, certainly; a racist like South Africa's Botha, of course; monsters like the terrorist groups, to be sure. But sorry about us? No, never. God could never be sorry that he has made you and me.

The result is that passages of Scripture such as our Old Testament lesson from Isaiah 28 become largely meaningless to us. Isaiah pictures here not only the destruction of Judah before the overwhelming flood of the Assyrian army but also the slow, inexorable tick-tock of God's judgments in the movement of time. Here a little, there a little—the Word of God destroying our life—bringing the gradual growth of fate, the monotonous stages of decay: ambition turned to empty envy, pride soured by loneliness and hatred, selfishness searching desperately for some new thing to feed its ego. God judges us in all the little things of life, says the prophet—in the terrible simplicity of every day. "Line upon line, here a little, there a little"—in the dissatisfactions that rob our peace and the troubles that disrupt our families, in the fears that come with a dark street at night, and the anxieties about our work on the morrow. Here a little, there a little, God's judgments work their way, until, in the words of Isaiah, we "go, and fall backward, and be broken, and snared, and taken."

But we resist that, don't we? We resist it, in the second place, because it disturbs our picture of God. At the deeper levels of faith, the portrayal of God as judge seems contrary to everything we have known about him—contrary to the love and mercy we have known from his hand all our life long, contrary to the grace we have experienced from him in the person of Jesus Christ. To say that the God of the cross is at the same time, in Hosea's figures, like a moth who eats away at the fabric of our life, or like dry rot who undermines our rickety foundations, is to call into question our entire understanding of the nature of the God we worship.

Isaiah acknowledges the difficulties with such a witness to God. When God works in wrath to do his deeds of judgment, says the prophet, those deeds are foreign to God's nature: "Strange is his deed. . . . alien is his work!" And yet, there is no softening of the message that follows that recognition:

> I have heard a decree of destruction
> from the Lord God of hosts upon the whole land.

Could it be that our God of love and mercy is also truly the Lord, and that he therefore will not be satisfied with anything less than the full worship in our lives of that lordship? When the heretical Marcion tried to eliminate the Old Testament's judgments from the canon and turn God

23

into a God of tender goodness only, Tertullian blasted Marcion's attack on God's lordship:

What a prevaricator of truth is such a god! What a dissembler with his own decisions. Afraid to condemn what he really condemns, afraid to hate what he does not love, permitting that to be done which he does not allow, choosing to indicate what he dislikes rather than deeply examine it! This will turn out an imaginary goodness, for the true God is not otherwise fully good than as an enemy of evil. . . .[6]

God is truly Lord, and he therefore judges our evil.

Surely the death—the real death—of Jesus Christ on the cross testifies to that fact. We may deny that God is judge and that he destroys our evil. But thanks be to God, his Son Jesus Christ did not share in our denial. Taking all our sin upon himself, he let it be done to death in his body. And thereby he testified that God is ruler of this world, who will not put up with evil. Sin has to die, if God is Lord: Jesus accepted that judgment. And he willingly gave his life for our sin to glorify God's lordship: "Now is my soul troubled. And what shall I say? 'Father, save me from this hour'? No, for this purpose I have come to this hour. Father, glorify thy name."

But that is not the last word of our text. The judgment of the cross was not God's last word, any more than was God's judgment in Isaiah's time. God's final glory, God's final lordship is that he kills only to make alive—he does away with our evil only to make us anew—he subjects us to his daily judgments to recreate us for an eternal love. In the midst of the overwhelming flood of wrath, sweeping over Judah, Isaiah sees the vision of a cornerstone of a new and faithful people of God, reestablished in Zion. And as Jesus Christ confronts the horror of being lifted up on the cross, he promises that that death will lead to eternal life for us all. "Now is the judgment of this world, now shall the ruler of this world be cast out; and I, when I am lifted up from the earth, will draw all men to myself."

So we do not reject the judgments of God. No, we do just

24

the opposite. We pray that our sin may be crucified, that we may be a new people, that we may enter into his good and eternal kingdom.

Amen.

Sample Meditation:

TIT FOR TAT?

Scripture: Romans 5:8-9 (Call to Worship)
Jonah 3-4

There is no more charming book within the Old Testament than the Book of Jonah. When we read it, we cannot help but smile over its angry little prophet, sulking under his castor oil plant. We cannot help but appreciate its imaginative characters—the good-hearted sailors, the great fish, the repentant Ninevite King and even cows, the worm, and the plant. Jonah is always good for at least a few chuckles, and we admire the artistry with which it was composed.

But if we really let the message of this little book get at us, we may take a different attitude toward Jonah altogether. In fact, we may even come to dislike the book thoroughly. For Jonah has some pertinent things to say about our attitudes toward justice in this world, and indeed, some hard things to say to our theology.

Jonah maintains that God can forgive and show mercy to anyone. Nineveh was the capital of the Assyrian empire, of course, and Assyria was the most rapacious and blood-thirsty nation of the ancient world. It had not only trampled and conquered every small nation along the Palestinian landbridge, but it had also plundered and spoiled their civilian populations and systematically deported them to other regions, so that the ten northern tribes of Israel had simply disappeared into its jaws, never to be heard from again in human history. And yet, this nation was the one to whom Jonah was sent to preach, and this murderer was the criminal whom the God of Judah forgave and spared. If you want to put it in modern terms, it was a little like forgiving Adolph Hitler. It's no wonder that the prophet Jonah was angry with God.

And we can identify with Jonah's anger, because we do not want mercy shown to those who deserve punishment for their deeds. We want them to suffer the full consequences of their evil actions. Take the Watergate criminals, for example. How easily all of them got off for their crimes against this nation, and now most of them are becoming rich by writing books about their experiences. Charles Colson even underwent a conversion experience, and now is looked to by many persons as a religious leader. Or take the average teen-age murderer in any big city. Because of his age, he usually gets tried in juvenile court, has his hands slapped, and in a few months is back on the street. There is something very upsetting about a system of justice like that. And if that's the way God works too, as the book of Jonah says it is, then we can share Jonah's outrage at such a blind application of mercy.

But let's bring the message down a little closer to home. How about all those persons with whom we violently disagree on religious matters? There they are, walking around, successful, happy, unconcerned, apparently quite satisfied with their own blind theological positions. How can God let them be so self-assured and joyful, when he knows how misguided they are and how much damage they are doing to the church? How about those persons who are undermining the causes we are trying to foster? By heaven, we wish they would get what's coming to them! Yes, you and I are very much like the prophet Jonah. We want some justice in this world and some evidence that God supports our views.

Of course we do have to take into account the fact that Nineveh repented. It never happened in actual history of course, but that's the way the story goes. Everyone in the wicked city turned and believed in God, from the king right on down to the lowliest peasant and even the cattle in the barnyard. Well, all right then, maybe God was justified in showing mercy to them. To be sure, they should have been held accountable for the evil they had done in the past. But they turned and believed in God, and so maybe they deserved his forgiveness. Maybe Charles Colson's conversion was real, and he can now be considered a religious person. Maybe if a criminal can be rehabilitated, he can be accepted back into society. And maybe if our wrong-headed opponents see the error of their ways, they, too, deserve our friendship and welcome into our fellowship. Yes, that's all right. That saves the book of Jonah. God forgives because a person repents. Tit for tat. Salvation for turning. There is a structure of justice after all. Maybe we modern-day Jonahs can learn to live with that, and gladly accept God's forgiveness of anyone who turns from his or her evil.

The interesting thing about the book of Jonah, however, is that the prophet himself never does repent, and yet, throughout the book, he is the constant recipient of God's mercy. Given the call to go to Nineveh, he sets out in exactly the opposite direction. Thrown overboard by the fearful sailors, Jonah nevertheless is saved by God by that fish. And then patiently, painstakingly, never in anger, God deals with his angry prophet, once again sending him to Nineveh—giving him success in his mission, overlooking his sulking, shading his head, working through worm and sun and explanation, to teach Jonah the marvels of mercy and the unlimited nature of love. Jonah does not repent, but God never gives up on him. And most of the time, we modern Jonahs do not repent either, but God does not give up on us. Instead, his Son goes to Jerusalem and dies a forgiving death for us that we do not deserve, and in his mercy, forgives our hatreds and prides and blind obstinacy.

God's love is not tit for tat, not the justice all us Jonahs have coming. No, while we are yet sinners, Christ dies for us. And for that reason, and that alone, you and I can live.

Amen.

Sample Meditation:

THE PURPOSE OF FORGIVENESS

Scripture: John 15:9-11 (Call to Worship)
Psalm 130 (Responsive Reading)
Romans 6:1-4, 12-14

On February 21, 1982, the Potomac Association of the United Church of Christ voted, by a margin of three to one, to ordain to the Christian ministry a practicing lesbian. Many of us fought against the decision, and when the vote was explained, one minister said, "It did not seem to be the loving thing to do to vote against her." I cite this incident because the statement of that minister is so symptomatic of our time: "It did not seem the loving thing to do to vote against her."

Above all else these days, we Christians want to be loving. We want to forgive. We want to accept people as they are. We want to offer them the unmerited love of Christ. Our Lord, we know, during his earthly life, accepted all sorts of unacceptable people. He taught us to forgive seventy times seven. But somehow we have forgotten Jesus' purpose for doing all those things. And so we have now come to the point in our society where, in the name of Christian love, we will accept almost any life-style and forgive almost any wrong. And in similar fashion, we expect to be accepted and forgiven, no matter how we live.

When a business aquaintance of ours in Pennsylvania left his wife and children and moved in with an assistant, his first words to his eldest child over the telephone were, "Do you forgive me?" He expected his actions to be accepted, though he fully intended to continue in them, just as we expect God to forgive us, though we fully intend to continue in our sin. It would, after all, not be the loving thing to do for God to vote against us.

The psalmist, in the passage that we read for our Old Testament lesson, however, has a different understanding of forgiveness. He too fully expects God to forgive his sin. Indeed, he assures his fellow worshipers that the Lord will redeem them from all their iniquities. But God's forgiveness, according to the psalmist, is not without its purpose: "There is forgiveness with thee," he says, "that thou mayest be feared." There is forgiveness with God in order that he may be served in awe and obedience. There is forgiveness with God in order that his acceptance of us may lead us to a new manner of living.

Paul, too, spells that out in the passage that we heard for our New Testament lesson. He asks the same question our careless society asks: "Can't we continue to sin that grace may abound? Can't we just continue in our old manner of life in order that God may just go on forgiving and forgiving and forgiving?" Paul replies, "By no means!" Then he spells out God's intention. We were baptized, he says—we were buried with Christ—we were forgiven through him, in order that we may walk in newness of life. God took us back again in order that we may keep his commandments, that we may respond in love to his love by living a life transformed by his power.

In other words, according to the Scriptures, any and all life-styles are not acceptable to this forgiving God of ours, and we do ourselves and other persons no favor when we pretend that they are. God wants obedience. God wants a loving response to his commandments, given us in Jesus Christ. And when an adulterous father asks his child, "Do you forgive me?" the proper Christian response to that is, "No, not unless you return home and put your adultery behind you."

Ah, how harsh and judgmental that sounds: to refuse a reconciliation with persons because they will not repent, because they seem determined to go on breaking the commandments of God. Aren't we being self-righteous when we take such an attitude? And wouldn't *we* want to be forgiven if we were the guilty father? The whole argument for rejection and judgment grates harshly on our modern ears and goes against the grain of our live-and-let-live age. We have lost any sense of moral outrage, you see, any sense of wrestling with the power of evil. We no longer even think we must desire to walk in newness of life before we can approach the Lord's table. And we certainly do not think it necessary to hurl an inkpot at the devil, as Luther did, in some strenuous sense of wrong. No, it is much easier to be accepting and forgiving and to live with human nature as it is, like Paul Tillich excusing his repeated faithlessness with the statement that he was simply manifesting the broken-ness of the human condition.

Only an age that really knows nothing about the mercy of God can treat forgiveness in such a manner, however, because God has an ultimate purpose in calling us to newness of life, and that final purpose is fully one of love. Above all else, God wants to give us a full and abundant life, but he also knows that we can have that life only if we walk by his commandments. As it is repeatedly said in Deuteronomy, these commandments are "for your good always." Or as in our call to worship from John, "These things I have spoken to you, that my joy may be in you, and that your joy may be full." Only the life-style that seeks God's will and surrenders to his guidance and power can enter into Christ's joy. He forgave us our sin that we may have that joy. We were baptized into his death that we may walk in his new life of obedience that brings with it more hope and happiness than ever we have imagined. That is what the forgiving love of God finally intends for us: transformed life, good life, our days lived out as they were meant to be, full of the gladness and satisfaction that only our Lord can give.

There *is* forgiveness with God, but it is given in order that he may be obeyed. And we are called to obey, in order that we may have joy. O Israel, put your hope in the Lord.

Amen.

B. Preaching about Poor and Rich, Oppressed and Oppressors

One of the major theological motifs in the Scriptures is God's prejudice on behalf of the poor and helpless.

Everywhere we find his special favor bestowed on the lowly and suffering of the world: in the Exodus, when he hears his people's cries and comes down to deliver them out of their slavery to their Egyptian overlords (Exodus 3:7-8); in the covenant law, which always stipulates protection for the stranger and the poor, the widow, and the orphan (Exodus 22:21-27; Leviticus 19:33f.; 25:35-37; Deuteronomy 24:10-15, 17-18; 27:19, etc.); in the prophets, who champion the cause of the weak over against the powers-that-be in their society (Amos 2:6-8; Ezekiel 34:1ff.; etc.); in the Psalms, whose righteous sufferers find their joy and security in God (e.g., Psalm 22); in the teachings of our Lord (e.g., Matthew 25:31ff.); and in the New Testament church (Acts 2:44-45; 6:1-6). Far from helping those who help themselves, God helps those who have no other helper, and it is the least in the world who will enter his kingdom first.

As a result, nothing eats at the consciences of American mainline churchgoers quite so much as their relative affluence and power over against most of the earth's population. The deuteronomic and Puritan belief that God rewards the righteous with material prosperity has, in our day, given way to widespread guilt over our possessions and influence, and such guilt has been newly fed by environmental and Third World movements. Indeed, some economic and political groups in the U.S. count on such guilt to foster continuing support for their causes.

A lot of rationalization takes place in the mind of the average churchgoer, however, when the preacher talks about money—rationalization powerful enough to prevent the churchgoer (and usually the preacher) from altering his or her life-style in any way. But the Christian gospel demands altered life-styles—walking by the Spirit and not by the flesh, in Paul's terminology. To foster that alteration, the preacher, therefore, has to be specific about what the new life in Christ involves, and that specificity has to be set within solid understandings of economic and political realities. It is often because preachers do not know much about economics and because they do not deal with the realities of living in the world, that many in their congregations do not listen to them.

On the other hand, a lot of romanticizing of the poor and oppressed also is practiced by churchgoers in this country, and the authority of the Bible for them often has been replaced by a humanistic, liberalistic gospel of charity and kindness that demands automatic allegiance to its social programs.

The two meditations that follow briefly examine these issues, from the biblical perspective.

Sample Meditation:

THE YELLOW BICYCLE

Scripture: Matthew 5:23-24 (Call to Worship)
Deuteronomy 15:7-11

Our worship in this place is always problematical. It is problematical because we are rich. We are among the haves of this world, you and I. We have plenty to eat, and clothes to wear, and a comfortable place to live, while all around us in this city and throughout the world, there are millions of have-nots. Therefore it is always a question when we enter this chapel as to whether or not God will accept the worship and hear the prayers of rich people like you and me. Jesus tells us that it is easier for a camel to go through the eye of a needle than it is for a rich person to enter the kingdom of God. So it is always a question when we come in here, possessing so much, whether or not God will allow us into his presence at all.

I think this was all brought home to me clearly last year in the incident of the yellow bicycle. Our family moved to Richmond just over a year ago, and when we moved, we bought each of our teen-aged children a new bicycle. They were beautiful Schwinn bikes—five-speed, with gleaming yellow paint and shining chrome, and our kids had a wonderful time getting to know their new hometown by riding their bikes around the city. When our son left for college, my husband used the bike to ride to the seminary each day, which saved fuel and provided my husband with exercise as well. He parked the yellow bicycle in the rack next to the library each day, locking it up with a standard and not too sturdy chain.

One afternoon late in October, the yellow bicycle was stolen from the rack, the chain severed by wire cutters and left lying on the ground. We were upset, to say the least. We reported the loss to the police and searched the neighborhood for some glimpse of the stolen bike. We had just about given up hope of recovering it, when we received a card from the police department: the bicycle had been found abandoned and was now at the police station. Joyfully we rushed downtown to retrieve our stolen property, only to have our gladness turned into dismay when we saw the condition of the bike. It had been systematically and viciously turned into a pile of junk. Apparently, whoever had stolen the bike was unable to keep it, and so the thief had slashed the seat with a knife and taken an ax or crowbar to the rest. Every piece on the formerly beautiful bicycle was now bent and marred. There was not one part that was salvageable. The yellow bicycle was good for nothing but the trash.

I kept that bike in the backyard for some days before I threw it away, however, and I wished at the time that I could somehow install it permanently on a pedestal in the seminary quadrangle—for it bore in its twisted frame the signs of an awful hatred: the hatred of one who could not have a bicycle and who decided we should not have one either, the hatred of one who in blind fury and rage had pounded a very minor symbol of affluence into useless junk, the hatred of one who had not, against all of us who have. It was totally unreasoning and destructive hatred to be sure, but it was also hatred that my family, and all of the rest of you affluent families, had instilled in someone's heart, simply by having what we have. Whoever stole that yellow bicycle probably still lives in Richmond, and he despises you and me, because compared to him, we are rich, and we have not shared our good fortune. He is one of the have-nots, on the outside looking in, at all of us wealthy haves in Richmond, who take our prosperity for granted.

Often when I come into this chapel to worship, I think about that yellow bicycle, and about the person who despised us so for having it. And then the words of our call to worship, from Jesus' Sermon on the Mount, come home to me, "If you are offering your gift at the altar, and there remember that your brother has something against you, leave your gift there before the altar and go; first be reconciled to your brother, and then come and offer your gift." Well, my brothers, the poor of this city, have an awful lot against me. How then do I dare to presume to come in here to worship? And our brothers, the poor of the world, cry out for food. How do we dare to pray when someone else is hungry? Surely, the answer can only be, "Through the mediation of Jesus Christ." But then the question arises: Are we using the death of our Lord as cheap grace, as an excuse not to help our brothers? And so the original questions come back: How do we dare to praise when millions behold the world with sunken eyes? How do we dare to sing when others can do nothing but weep?

Those are terrible questions for us affluent and comfortable Americans, at least for us citizens who call ourselves Christians. And I do not know the answer to the questions. I only know that we who bear the name of Christ must continue to give and give freely, through our churches and local charities, even when the world's needs are so great that giving seems to do no more good. I only know that in this time of inflation and depression, when social programs and welfare are the first to be cut out of government budgets, we who confess Christ as Lord must continue to insist that part of city and state and national budgets go to help the poor. And above all, I only know that when we come into this chapel to pray, we who have so much stand condemned before the judge of our lives, who has made us responsible for our brothers' welfare. As long as another hungers and we eat, we are guilty before our God, and there is only one prayer that is initially possible to any of us: "Lord, be merciful to me—a sinner."

Amen.

Sample Meditation:

ON ROMANTICIZING THE POOR AND OPPRESSED

Scripture: Jeremiah 5:1-6

One of the functions of Scripture in the Christian faith is continually to correct the church—to bring its thinking and actions back into line with the apostolic faith. And certainly nowhere is this more necessary today than with our attitudes toward the rich and the poor, the oppressors and the oppressed.

It is probably true to say that no one in this room considers the rich of this world to be righteous. No—we have learned our lessons well. We know it is easier for a camel to go through the eye of a needle than for a rich man to enter the kingdom of heaven. We know that it was poor Lazarus, begging at the door, who ended up in the bosom of Abraham, while the rich man in Jesus' parable suffered torment in Hades. We know that the love of money is the root of all evil, and that our Lord came to preach good news to the poor. Therefore we are not surprised by our Old Testament lesson when Jeremiah finds, in his search for one righteous man in Judah, that there is no such person to be found among the rich and the great. Rich and powerful persons, by definition, cannot be numbered among the righteous.

But we are not too sure about the poor and oppressed. Are they not, because of their condition, the most beloved of the Lord? Jesus himself taught us that the lowly of the earth would enter the kingdom of God before us. Do they not, therefore, have about them an innate rightness in the eyes of their God, a purity of soul, an innocence of thought, which we well-to-do people cannot match? And should we not therefore look to them for true understanding of the gospel? Should we not consider their ways the right ways to live in this world?

Certainly many persons in the church have thought so. Some years ago James Cone stated that it was impossible for an oppressed person to sin. And recently Catherine and Justo Gonalez have suggested in a book on liberation preaching that the only way truly to understand the New Testament is to understand it from the standpoint of the poor. In similar fashion, if a group can show it is among the oppressed of this world, then it takes upon itself a certain self-righteousness. Its statements about how the church should think and act in this world become authoritative, and so we find ourselves hesitating to challenge a Third World mission report, or a feminist theology, or a Gray Panther proclamation, while at the same time we feel guilty inside because we do not wholeheartedly agree with them. We think that we do not enthusiastically support their claims to righteousness and justice and truth because of our own sinfulness.

The interesting fact, however, is that our Scripture passage from Jeremiah does not attribute such good qualities to the poor and oppressed. On the contrary, Jeremiah says, "They have made their faces harder than rock; they have refused to repent." And the whole Bible agrees with that statement. "None is righteous; no, not one," proclaims Paul, quoting the psalmist. "All have sinned and fall short of the glory of God." And so it is poor fisherman, the disciples of Jesus, who never understand him and who flee from his cross, just as it is a group of lowly-born, ignoble and unlearned Corinthians who disrupt the first century church. In short, it is all persons—be they poor or rich, unlearned or learned, weak or powerful, oppressed or ruthless—who stand guilty before the judgment of God. And the amazing thing about the grace of God toward the poor and helpless is not that they deserve it—any more than we do—but that God's favor toward them totally contradicts the way the world has treated them.

God's mercy and favor are always unearned, no matter to whom they are given, and there can be as much selfishness and sinful pride found in an old folks' home as are found among corporation executives. There can be as much error in a feminist or liberation or Third World theology as in one formulated by white, male Americans. There can be as much greed roaming loose on the streets of a ghetto as in the trading centers of Wall Street.

None is righteous—no, not one. That's a hard truth from the Scriptures. But it is also a truth that we need very much to absorb, because it has implications for our calling both as theologians and as evangelists.

You see, we can never learn our theological wisdom from the wisdom of this world, and the viewpoint of every group, no matter who they may be, must be subjected to the searching light of the Scriptures. Countless people these days are being led astray by bad theology, and we need to point out that badness. To be sure, some of the followers of the ideologies we attack may be outraged, and we may be subjected to scorn. But our Lord never promised it would be easy to proclaim the gospel.

Second, let me not be misunderstood: we are most assuredly sent by God to minister to the poor, to free the captives, to bind up the brokenhearted, to bring good news to those who are helpless. But we must never forget that part of the good news, for them as well as for us, is the moral power of the gospel, meant to transform their characters and actions as surely as it transforms ours. Some of the radical feminists and some of the residents of old folks' homes, who simply wallow in self-pity, are not to be left with the belief that such selfishness is acceptable. The poor are not to be told, as they were told a couple of years ago in Richmond, that it is all right to steal. The oppressed are not to be left with the impression that they can do anything they please, once they are freed. God in Jesus Christ changes lives, total lives—ethical, physical, spiritual—and you and I are heralds of that life-transforming gospel. None of us is righteous—no, not one. But God is. And his righteous grace toward all people, irrespective of condition or status, is to make of them and us, in Jesus Christ, totally new creations.

Amen.

C. Preaching about God's Work in Nature

One of the most difficult tasks for many preachers is that of relating God's actions to the natural world. We live in a scientific age and in a culture that have a largely secularized world view. That is, most Americans consider the universe, with all its huge and numerous galaxies, to be a closed system operating entirely by natural laws, apart from any influence of God upon it. If one of those natural laws is disrupted, faithful churchgoers may label such an occurrence a miracle and believe that God has caused it. They may believe that miracles happened frequently in biblical times and that they occasionally happen today. But most of the time, even the faithful consider Nature an entity apart from God, rolling on in its course, bestowing its bounties or wreaking its havoc, quite apart from God's intentions and actions.

Therefore the Christian doctrine of creation remains intact for most mainline Christians as only a rather vague and general statement of the origin of themselves and of their world—and perhaps the blurred nature of the doctrine for most has been evidenced recently in the nationwide, nonsensical arguments over "creationism." On the other hand, the Bible's testimonies to God as sole sustainer of his creation and to the total dependence of the natural world upon his will have become incomprehensible for many. Few modern churchgoers in our largest denominations could agree with the thought of Psalm 104 or Amos 4:6-12 or Isaiah 40:21-22, or even Matthew 6:25-33 or John 1:3.

If we truly believe that God is Lord of nature as well as of history, Christian preachers must be able to point to his work in the natural world. But that pointing must be done carefully, to prevent the natural religion and Baal worship against which the whole Bible, and especially Genesis 1 and Deuteronomy and the prophets, fight.

The following meditation is an example of one such pointer.

Sample Meditation:

SEASONS' MEANING

Scripture: Genesis 6:5-8; 8:20-22

Richmond is a beautiful city, and it is difficult to say at what season it is the most beautiful—whether in the spring, when the sight of azaleas and dogwoods causes us to catch our breath at every turn, or now in the fall, when the maples glow in red and golden glory. We here on the northside are presented with a magnificence in the march of the seasons, which inspires even the busiest among us to stop and look and exclaim. And the question arises, therefore, as to how we should look at these wonders of seasonal beauty. Certainly we should enjoy them and appreciate them and marvel at them, but even the atheists and pagans do that, and we have to ask if there is not a special way in which we Christians should regard the world around us.

It is not as simple a question as it may seem, for we Americans have always had a great deal of difficulty in coming to terms with the natural world. Most of the time, as urban dwellers, we simply ignore nature—until God sets one of his trees on fire with color and demands that we take notice of it. Other times we idealize nature—our dime store art testifies to that—and we refuse to recognize that the natural world is a realm of blood and fang and claw. In these times of great interest in ecology, we know that we have often considered the created world as simply an object to be manipulated with our technology. And worst of all, we have all, at some time or another, worshiped the natural world, supposedly finding God in its peace and beauty, mistakenly lifting up our eyes to the hills—as if somehow God were revealed in the eternal hills instead of in his Son Jesus Christ.

So it is not a simple question when we ask how we should regard the autumn splendors outside this chapel, but perhaps our Scripture lesson for the morning can help us with the answer.

At the beginning and end of the flood story in Genesis,

the Yahwist has provided us with two speeches of the Lord. The first of these speeches shows us the Creator of this world sobbing over his creation, because every "imagination of the thoughts of [our] heart" is only evil continually. You see, you and I do not know how to live in God's good creation. We scheme—we scheme how to get ahead in the world. In an attitude of what we consider to be great responsibility and wisdom, we carefully map out our day-to-day work and our own plans for the future. We calculate what we must do to secure a comfortable living standard. We cultivate the friendship of those who are important, and ignore the weak and unimportant. We make ourselves the center of the world, and do everything to promote our own cause. And that, our Scripture lesson says, grieves God to his heart. His reaction to our selfish attempts to run our own lives, apart from concern for him and our neighbor, is not wrath, but an aching heart and weeping over his children. As God weeps over Israel in the prophecies of Hosea, and Jesus weeps over Jerusalem in the gospel story, so the creator of this season of autumn weeps over us, because we do not love him and our neighbor, but only our own selves.

That means that God really should destroy us now, as he destroyed his creation in the days of Noah. He is sorry that he has made you and me. We really have not turned out as he wanted us to be. We have not at all lived up to his intentions for us. And so, according to our text, our end should be annihilation. God, in his grief, should do away with us and just start all over again.

But there is an amazing turn in the second part of our Scripture readings, which changes everything for you and me. The human race does not improve after the salvation of Noah and his family from the flood. The "imagination of the thoughts of [our] heart" are still evil "from our youth." Even when we are pious members of this congregation, even when we serve the church, even when we think we do good, we are still unworthy servants. Despite all our faith and ethical living, we are still self-centered children, running away from our Father and grieving him to his heart.

Despite our continuing sin even after his salvation of us, we are told in this second text from Genesis that God does not wipe us out once for all. Instead he forgives and finally responds to our faithlessness simply with a promise: "Neither will I ever again destroy every living creature as I have done. While the earth remains, seedtime and harvest, cold and heat, summer and winter, day and night, shall not cease."

That promise of forgiveness for all our sin was made real for us in Jesus Christ. There in the cross and resurrection, God manifested the mercy that now preserves us and our world, despite all our wrong against him. And the change of the seasons is an outward sign of God's redemption of us through his Son. Instead of punishing us for the weeping we constantly cause him, God turns the maples to red and gold. Instead of casting us out from his presence, he brings the birds south for the winter. Instead of sending us into darkness, he gives us a harvest moon, and causes the stars to shine with special brightness in the crisp cold of autumn nights.

The season has moved into fall, and now the winter lies ahead, and after that the glory of spring and the heat of summer, because our God is merciful—because his response to our rebellion against him is not destruction of us, and death, but in Jesus Christ the loving preservation of everything he has made. "While the earth remains, seedtime and harvest, cold and heat, summer and winter, day and night, shall not cease." God sealed that promise with his Son.

And so how should we look at the world around us? Surely we should marvel and enjoy and exclaim. But above all, we should praise our Creator who, in Jesus Christ, has made this autumn—and every season—the manifestation of his marvelous mercy.

Amen.

D. Preaching the Kingdom of God

One of the central messages of the New Testament, which is now rarely heard by the average churchgoer, is the proclamation of the coming of the kingdom of God in the person of Jesus Christ. That coming kingdom was promised in every major theological complex in the Old Testament. Hexateuchal theology looked forward to the time when all the families of the earth would be blessed through God's chosen instrument—Israel, the descendants of Abraham (Genesis 12:3). Royal theology anticipated the coming of the righteous King, who would rule by the Spirit of the Lord (Isaiah 11:1ff.) and reign over a universal and peaceful realm (Zechariah 9:9-10). The prophets promised the new age of the kingdom, on the other side of the judgment of the exile, with a new exodus (Isaiah 52:11-12) and wilderness wanderings (Isaiah 48:20-21) to a renewed promised land (Ezekiel 34:25-31), where Israel would dwell in faithfulness and security, in a new covenant relation with her God (Jeremiah 31:31-34), and would, by her light, attract all nations into her fellowship (Isaiah 60:1-3; 56:6-8). Israel anticipated that coming kingdom and knew a foretaste of it in her worship (Psalms 47, 96-99). Throughout most of the pages of the Old Testament, she strains forward toward its arrival.

When Jesus of Nazareth appeared, announcing that the kingdom of God was at hand in him (Mark 1:14-15; Luke 11:20, 17:21), the hopes of all the years of Israel's expectations were realized (cf. Luke 2:29-32, 36-38; 24:21) and then finally confirmed by Christ's resurrection (Luke 24:21-35). Paul was convinced that the new age of the kingdom had begun (e.g., 2 Corinthians 5:16-6:2), that the powers of the old age had been defeated (e.g., Romans 6:5-23), and that the church had the first fruits of the fullness of the kingdom in the presence of the Spirit with it (e.g., Romans 8:23; Galatians 5:22-24). Indeed, the Deutero-Pauline letters went beyond that to state that the church lived already in the kingdom of God (cf. Colossians 1:13-14; Ephesians 2:6-8; Hebrews 12:28-29).

Such scriptural teaching has almost totally dropped out of the preaching of the major denominations. In short, we no longer have any form of "realized eschatology," which acknowledges that the new age has already begun to come and that the church can live in newness of love and life because it is given the powers of the new age by the Spirit. Our eschatology, in so far as we have any, is entirely future and deals almost exclusively with the gift of eternal life after death.

Both the charismatic movement and the pentecostal sects have taken up the neglected message of the presence of the powers of the kingdom in our midst, and it is their preaching of the very real power given by Christ in the Spirit that is partly responsible for the success of their communities. We mainline preachers, on the other hand, shy away from their triumphalism and emphasize, perhaps at far too much length, the persistence and depth of human sin.

If we do wish to preach the New Testament's message of the arrival of the kingdom in Jesus Christ, however, we have to ask where and how that kingdom is present in our world. Certainly we occasionally glimpse its glory in worship, and the Lord's Supper is always a foretaste of the final messianic banquet. But beyond that, where are the evidences of the kingdom come? The following meditation makes only a brief beginning at answering that question.

Sample Meditation:

THE KINGDOM COME

Scripture: 2 Corinthians 6:2 (Call to Worship)
Isaiah 61:1-3, Luke 4:14-21

One of the things that impresses me most about our Old Testament lesson in Third Isaiah is how unbelievable it must have sounded to those who heard it for the very first time. This oracle does nothing less than announce the coming of the kingdom of God on earth—the year of the Lord's favor to Judah. As the passage continues, it promises that all of Judah's ancient ruins will be built up, that she shall eat the wealth of nations, that she shall have everlasting joy, and that all peoples will flow to her, to serve her, and to worship her God.

But this message was proclaimed in the sixth century B.C. to a struggling, little province that was nothing more than a captured people in the Persian empire. Judah's land was in ruins; her king and temple were gone; her economic situation was desperate; her society was infested with widespread injustice and idolatry. There was no reason whatsoever for the inhabitants of Judah to believe that this announcement would change any of their circumstances, for the truth is that they had heard it all before and none of it had come true.

Earlier Second Isaiah had made Judah glowing promises about the coming of the kingdom, and none of it—not one word of it—had really come to pass. Oh sure, Cyrus had let them return to Palestine, but for what? For nothing except poverty and captivity and hearts broken by bad news and affliction.

Besides, these words were being spoken to Judah by a despised little bunch of Levites and prophets, who either had been ousted from their jobs or generally discredited by the community. The Judeans probably put no more faith in this message than we would put in that of some ragged figure, walking our city streets, carrying a sign saying, Repent, the Kingdom Is at Hand. The announcement of the coming of the kingdom was totally absurd for Judah.

It was also absurd for the inhabitants of Nazareth in Jesus' day. Our Lord claimed to fulfill this prophecy from Third Isaiah. He stood up in his hometown synagogue one day and read the words from the first two verses of Isaiah 61. And when he had closed the book, he said to them, "Today this Scripture has been fulfilled in your hearing." And that is comforting for us, of course, because it reassures us that the Word of God actually does come true. But it didn't reassure the residents of Nazareth at all. If the kingdom of God had come in their midst, they wanted evidence of it, and when Jesus refused to give them evidence, they tried to kill him by throwing him off a cliff outside of town. Jesus escaped their wrath, and when we read the story in Luke, we think how foolish the people in Nazareth were, not to believe that the kingdom of God had actually come into

44

their midst. How foolish they were, not to understand that Third Isaiah's words had been fulfilled!

But have they been fulfilled? Has the kingdom really come into your life and mine? The announcement here in Third Isaiah's words is of good tidings to the poor, binding up of the broken hearted, freedom for all who are captive, joy for those who mourn, and revitalization for all who are weak and despairing of life. Have those good things actually come into this world as we know it? Or are poverty, devastation, injustice, and idolatry still very real facts of life, and are these words of Third Isaiah actually as empty of meaning for us as they were for the inhabitants of post-exilic Judah? Where is the evidence of the coming of the kingdom of God? Where is the proof of God's working? Where are the certain signs that God has ever kept this prophetic word?

When our daughter was in college, she was a member of the Brown University chorus, and one December in Lincoln Center in New York, we saw a remarkable movie of a trip that some members of that chorus had made to India. One of the stops on the chorus' itinerary was at Mother Theresa's hospital for the dying in Calcutta. There, before an audience made up of the emaciated forms of the poor, the starving, the disease-ridden, the outcast—all lying in bed waiting for death—the Brown University chorus sang Randall Thompson's magnificent anthem, "Allelujah." Tears ran down the students' faces as they sang, but one could well have asked them, How can you sing "Allelujah" in such a setting? Where is there any cause at all for praise in the wards of such human misery? How can you sing the Lord's song in such a situation of suffering? Surely "Allelujah" belongs in the kingdom of God, not among the dregs of the dying!

And yet, a remarkable result followed the singing of that song. When the notes of that anthem of praise died away in that hospital for death, every bony face on every hospital pillow shone forth with some glimpse of a transforming glory. And the dying smiled and laughed and held out arms of love to those college students.

Could it be that the kingdom of God actually has begun to

come on this earth, in Jesus Christ, and we have simply missed seeing it? Could it be that these words of Third Isaiah really have been fulfilled and that is the reason they have been preserved for us all these centuries? Could it be that wherever these words have been proclaimed, they have *in fact* come to broken-hearted and captive people as good news, and have *in truth* transformed lives and unloosed bonds and given new hope and life? And could it be that those who have understood these words, as Mother Theresa understands them, have indeed always gone out in the name of Christ to minister to the poor and to comfort those who mourn and to give new life to the dying?

God always keeps his promises, good Christians. The year of the Lord's favor is upon us. "Now is the acceptable time. Now is the day of salvation." The kingdom of God is *in fact* in our midst in Jesus Christ, our Lord. And so today this Scripture has been fulfilled in our hearing also. Blessed are those who hear the good news and who go out and do it.

Amen.

E. Preaching One Holy Catholic Church

It has been said in recent times that the ecumenical movement is dead. Certainly such a general statement is far too sweeping. While some national and international ecumenical organizations have incurred much disfavor, others have prospered and continued their interdenominational conversations and cooperation. While some denominations have been rent by schism, others have entered or are planning new mergers.

Nevertheless, there is a certain spirit of partisanship abroad in the land, as there always is when church bodies find themselves under attack. The Christian faith is threatened in this country primarily by syncretism. There is an easy acceptance among the members and clergy of some churches of alien doctrines, non-Christian life-styles, and secular authorities. When this happens, traditional Christian churches often draw into themselves, restate their basic beliefs, and shun cooperation with those outside their circle. Their intent becomes to guard the purity of the gospel—a purpose clearly seen also in the pastoral and Johannine epistles of the New Testament.[7]

Such stewarding of the purity of the gospel is a legitimate function of church theology. At the same time, the danger is that such partisanship will lead to doctrinal exaggeration, provincial narrowness, and class hatreds, which deny the very gospel they are trying to protect. There is one holy, catholic (universal) body of Christ, which must be affirmed from the Christian pulpit, year in and year out, even in the midst of controversy. Indeed, the one hope of the church in its controversies is that it is, nevertheless, one in Christ Jesus.

Ecumenism remains healthy only insofar as it finds its center in its Lord. The following meditation reaffirms that center.

Sample Meditation:

THE RICHES OF THE CHURCH

Scripture: Ephesians 3:1-19

"To me . . . was given, to preach to the Gentiles the unsearchable riches of Christ."

Paul's vision of the church was the direct result of his vision of Jesus Christ, and because he knew Christ was boundless, he knew the church could have no boundaries imposed upon it by human beings.

Listen to the descriptions of the working of God in Christ Jesus that flood the pages of Ephesians, as the author piles phrase on phrase to tell of the wealth that has flowed out to us in our Lord: God's purpose in Christ, he says, is a "plan for the fulness of time, to unite all things in him, things in heaven and things on earth" (1:10). And so God in Christ has poured out on the church his "manifold wisdom" (3:10), "the riches of his glorious inheritance" (1:18), "the immeasurable greatness of his power" (1:19), "the working of his great might" (1:19), "the immeasurable riches of his grace in kindness" (2:7), "the riches of his glory" (3:16), the breadth and length and height and depth of the love of Christ (3:19f), which is the very "fulness of God" (3:19).

Is it any wonder, then, that for Paul the church could not be limited? It formed the body of Jesus Christ, whose grace could not be measured, and therefore for Paul, the church could have no human limit set upon it. It could not be reserved only for the Judaizers and those who followed the law; it had to spread out to the ends of the earth and include Gentiles as well. It could not be made up only of those who spoke in tongues or who had one gift of the Spirit; it had to manifest the many gifts of the Spirit of Christ poured out upon it. It could not be the domain of only males or free, because immeasurable mercy had been offered in Christ to females and slaves as well. There was no way one part of the body of Christ could say to another, "We have no need of you," because the inexhaustible riches of Christ had flowed out to all who confessed his name. And that flood would continue to swell until Christ was all in all, and all things in heaven and earth had been united together in him. Ephesians may have been written by a disciple of Paul, rather than the apostle himself, but it certainly is the direct consequence of Paul's universal vision. To him was given to preach to the Gentiles the unsearchable riches of Christ.

We sitting in this chapel are the heirs of that vision of the church. Because Paul could see beyond the boundaries of his own little world, because he was freed from the limitations of his own backyard, because he lifted up his eyes to see beyond the borders of his own region of Palestine and Syria, to Asia Minor and Greece and even Spain, because he knew it would take the whole world to fill out the body of Christ, the church moved west to evangelize Europe, and the British Isles, and finally America. And you and I are the heirs of that mission and the recipients of the glorious good news of the gospel.

But the question that confronts us is this: Will we now deny the broadness of the vision that brought us into the church in the first place? You see, there are those in our day who would like to limit the body of Christ—who would like to say that they preach Christ, but that he must be a Presbyterian Christ or a United Church Christ or a Baptist Christ or a charismatic Christ or a Moral Majority Christ. They would like to limit their people's vision of the church to only what is Reformed or Lutheran or Roman Catholic, or, worst of all, the latest fad. Or they would identify the unsearchable riches of Christ with the theological gems of a particular tradition or movement, and ignore the vast treasures of two thousand years of church history.

And the question is, can we in good conscience, make Christ so small again? Do we really want to teach our people that, contrary to Paul's magnificent vision, Christ's body now has a limit on it, and that it now consists of only one arm and a part of a foot, or maybe two or three fingers? Or worse still, do we want to claim that our part of the body makes up the whole, and that there is no other reality to the church than what people see in us? Do we want to claim that we show forth the breadth and length and height and depth of all that is Jesus Christ? Do we seriously believe that we manifest the fullness of his glory? And that the world can now find in our tradition alone the unsearchable riches of his grace? Heaven help us if we make that claim for ourselves, for the we have truly lost our vision, and the Christ we preach will be a very small Christ indeed!

No, the Christian church, the body of Christ, is as full and rich as its head, and therefore it is made up of hundreds of different worship forms and traditions. The body of Christ is the Greek Orthodox with their mystery and mysticism and their communion of saints across the ages. The body of Christ is the Roman Catholics, with their deep knowledge of the channels of grace. The body of Christ is the Lutheran at mass and the Reformed searching his Scriptures. The body of Christ is the Mennonite, lifting hymns of peace in a cappella song, and the Moravian with his brass choir, celebrating the love feast. The body of Christ is the black Baptist, dancing out his praise, and the Quaker waiting quietly for the illumination of the inner light. The body of Christ is all those of every tradition, who confess that Jesus Christ is Lord. It is that universal fellowship, which is as wide as the love of its Master, which is as varied as the workings of his mercy, and which is as richly multitudinous as the unsearchable riches of his grace.

Into such a body we have been baptized, and of that one body you and I are members. And the fullness of its life is ours to know and to taste, to cherish and to appreciate. Let no one limit the Christian church, and let no one give it bounds, except that of confessing that Jesus Christ is its living Lord and that we are his servants.

Then indeed the fullness of the life of our Lord may be made manifest through his body, and the world may finally come to know that his love has no limits on it. To Paul—and to us—has been given the task of making known to the world the unsearchable riches of Christ. Let no one diminish the treasure, until all are united in him.

Amen.

Part Two

PREACHING AS THEOLOGY AND ART

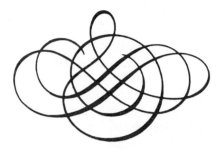

P reaching is a form of oral communication but as such, it need not necessarily be an art form. There are all sorts of oral communications that have no artistry about them whatsoever: telephone conversations, chats with neighbors, parental commands to children, even many public speeches. No one would maintain that the speeches of President Jimmy Carter, for example, were artistic. They lacked certain qualities in their content and delivery that prevented them from deserving the label of "art." On the other hand, few people would hesitate to give the title of art to the speeches of Prime Minister Winston Churchill during World War II. What was the difference in the oral communications of these two leaders, or more to the point, what turns an ordinary speech or sermon into an artistic creation?

Surely the answer is that art allows the one seeing or hearing it to enter into a new experience. A painter puts colors on canvas in such a way that his viewers are enabled to see what he sees and to participate in reality in a new way. A poet arranges words in such a manner that they convey to their hearers a new look at the world—the words become transparent to a new perception of reality. So too in the art of preaching: the English language is framed in such a way that the congregation is allowed to enter into a new experience—to exchange their old perceptions of themselves, their world, and God for new perceptions, to step outside an old manner of life and see the possibility of a new one. In the words of Paul, they are to "not be conformed to this world," but to "be transformed by the renewal of [their] minds."

There are many different elements involved in that transforming art of preaching. I have spelled them out in detail in my book, *Creative Preaching*.[8] Briefly, these elements include the ability of the preacher to shape a sermon into an organic whole, along a consistent line of thought; to make every paragraph vivid and concrete and clear by the use of imagery and metaphors and illustrations; to keep the congregation's experience of the text moving steadily toward a planned goal and response, without letting them bog down at some point or wander aside along the way; to allow the hearers to live into the biblical text and to make it a part of their lives. Those are all well-known characteristics of good preaching, and they have been detailed in countless books on homiletics. Moreover, such elements of homiletical art have been mastered by many preachers in this country.

Yet, I think it is true to say that preaching at the present time is rarely artistic, because many preachers, while good journeymen, have not become true masters of the English language. Involved in the artistic use of English are timing and rhythm and sound, and many preachers have no knowledge of the importance of these characteristics of speech for riveting attention and carrying along a congregation and touching their hearts as well as their minds. It is rare in homiletics classes, for example, to find a student who knows something about the rhythm of speech, and who therefore chooses one word instead of another to preserve the cadence of a sentence. It is equally rare to find a preacher who uses alliteration or onomatopoeia or assonance, or who knows that the sounds of some words in the English language are more pleasing than others. But the cadence of a sentence draws a congregation into it, and certain sounds elicit certain emotions. These are fine points in the art of preaching not often found in our pulpits. Nor are there many preachers who vary the length of sentences for the purpose of emphasis, or who break up the flow of a long narrative by the use of an illustration, or who have mastered timing in writing and delivery with stops and starts and changes in rhythm. It is such mastery of the English language in preaching that gives it the quality of true art.

This implies, of course, that every preacher should read extensively in the best literature, in order to absorb its style. It also implies that every preacher should practice, practice, his or her writing and speaking, until words have become the sharply-honed tools that they were given us to be.

No preacher should imagine, however, that rhetorical mastery is the sole key to fine preaching. Reinhold Niebuhr once wrote in his parish diary that he had vowed never to preach "pretty sermons," and some have quoted that statement of Niebuhr's as an excuse for their lack of eloquence in the pulpit. But Niebuhr was not talking about true art in homiletics; no one was more able to confront the world in which he lived with the gospel than was Reinhold Niebuhr. Rather, Niebuhr was talking, as he usually talked, about the exercise of human pride. "Pretty sermons," to his mind, engaged in high-flown rhetoric for rhetoric's sake. They used learned illustrations to show off the preacher's cleverness. They employed arresting imagery, but never witnessed to God. They dealt with topics that bore no relation to the biblical text. And Niebuhr would have leveled the New Testament's judgment against those preachers who so exercised their pride: "Verily . . . they have their reward." That is, preachers who rely on rhetoric alone and who never preach God's word may be famed as orators, but their people go away still hungry and thirsty, unfed by the "bread from heaven" and without "the water of eternal life."

As we attempt to improve our homiletical skills, we preachers also have to bear in mind that finally each one of us is dependent on God's Holy Spirit, and that no rhetorical device, be it ever so sophisticated, can capture the working of that Spirit. God, in his free grace, brings home to the hearts of our people his word, when and where he wills. He alone determines when and how he will act among his covenant folk. "I will be gracious to whom I will be gracious," he has told us, "and will show mercy on whom I will show mercy" (Exodus 33:19). No artistic skill in our preaching can command his sovereign working.

Yet, we preachers have been called to proclaim the word of God, and if we do nothing else, we should at least prepare the way for the Lord to come to our people. By the language we use, we should remove every stone of misunderstanding over which our congregations may stumble—free them from every low bog of ignorance and from every high prison tower of indifference, shake every sleeping soul awake who has not been watchful, and comfort every anxious person who waits with the fear that the Lord will never come. Then we have the glad word to announce as Deutero-Isaiah announced it: "Behold, your God! Behold, the Lord God comes . . ." (Isaiah 40:9-10). Surely that total task should draw from us the highest skill we have to offer!

The development of the art of preaching, however, is also—once again—a matter of mastering the church's theology. It is no accident that some of the church's greatest theologians have also been among her finest preachers, for theology, too, lends its contribution to the art of preaching. Indeed, the preacher who is most firmly grounded in the biblical, theological tradition of the church is also the preacher who is most able to preach with vividness, clarity, power, and eloquence. Those theological schools that have designed their homiletics departments primarily as departments of speech and communication have misunderstood the basic nature of preaching.

The preacher who is rooted and grounded in the biblical, theological tradition of the church—who has made that tradition part and parcel of his or her own being—is the preacher who understands the gospel. And it is a truism that the person who most thoroughly understands a subject

54

is the one who can explain and describe it most simply and clearly. Students sometimes hem and haw over theology, with the excuse, "I understand it, but I can't explain it." Nonsense! Words lie at the basis of all thought processes, and to know is to be able to articulate. Indeed, the better a subject is known, the more clearly it can be presented orally. One has the haunting suspicion that we often get opaque and confusing sermons in this country, not because their preachers are inadequately trained in speech, but because they are inadequately trained in theology. They do not understand the Christian faith and therefore cannot proclaim it.

By the same token, a preacher who is thoroughly versed in the biblical, theological tradition of the church is the one who can make the gospel most vivid—who can apply it to everyday life, in the colors and sights and sounds and smells and feelings of ordinary human existence. The reason for that is quite simple: the preacher has daily applied the gospel to his or her own existence. He or she has wrestled with the problems and perplexities, the ambiguities and sufferings involved in trying to live the Christian life in our society. That wrestling then gets embodied in the illustrations the preacher uses—in the concreteness of the preacher's words—in the imagery of the preacher's language. No abstract theological language and no unrealistic Pollyannaism for one who tries to live the Christian faith! Faith's demands and judgments, its sustenance and mercy become vividly real when it is practiced, and that realism and that vividness then permeate the sermon.

Again, the preachers who have absorbed Bible and church theology into their own bones are the preachers who can proclaim the Christian message powerfully, because they themselves have been made recipients of the power of the gospel. They live and move and have their being in an effectual Word that has exercised its power in their lives and in the lives of their congregations. They themselves have been forgiven, despite all their sin; they themselves have become new creatures in Christ by God's reconciling action. More than that, time and time again, they have seen God's recreative power at work in the lives of their people. They have seen God's might at work, giving some parishioner a new beginning by wiping out the past. They have watched God wrest victory from the defeat of some lay person. They have witnessed hope restored when some situation has seemed hopeless. They have seen death turned into life and a cause for rejoicing. With II Timothy they can say, "I know whom I have believed" (1:12), and that sure knowledge lends to preaching the power to proclaim the working Word, and to proclaim it, moreover, with a contagious conviction and commitment.

Finally, the preacher who stands firmly in the theology of Bible and of church is the herald who can speak with eloquence, because God's character is personally known. When you know God personally, it becomes quite clear that timid, faltering, weak words are inadequate to testify to his glory—for his presence bestows on us not "a spirit of timidity, but a spirit of power and love and self-control." How can you testify to a God who "calls out all the stars by name" except with poetry and grandeur and eloquence? How can you portray the "clouds and thick darkness and fire" that accompany his holiness except in words freighted with awe and mystery? How can you make comprehensible that he hears our cries or weeps over our indifference or pledges good to us with "all his heart and soul," except in phrases of unequaled tenderness? How can you portray his victory shout on Easter morn apart from words that trumpet his rule? Preachers who are church theologians know their God. The Lord has been revealed to them through the mediation of the Bible and of the churchly testimony to its Word that spans twenty centuries. Such preachers are heirs of the unsearchable riches of Christ, handed on by the church's faithful witnesses, and those riches have become the theologians' own property—a never-exhausted store of wonder, to which they know they must unceasingly give eloquent expression.

All of this is not to say that church theologians are automatically heir to the artistry of preaching. They have to work at it like anyone else. But they have an indispensable foundation upon which to build, and apart from that foundation there is no possibility of being an adequate, much less an eloquent, preacher.

To be sure, to cultivate the art of preaching, seminary students first must be trained in Bible. They must have a thorough knowledge and appropriation of the contents and varying theologies found in the Scriptures. They must have skill in exegesis and exposition of biblical passages. And contrary to the practice in many theological schools, those passages must be understood not only as historical records, but also primarily as Holy Scripture—that is, as the living Word of God that creates and sustains and guides the church's life, through the Holy Spirit.

But beyond that, seminary students must also be trained in the church's theology—not in philosophical theology or theoretical theology, but in the church's traditional theology. To foster that education, Dr. John Leith, distingished Reformed theologian at Union Theological Seminary in Richmond, Virginia, once drew up a list of the minimum requirements for training seminary students to do constructive work in theology. Those of non-Reformed communions would certainly make some changes in Leith's recommendations, especially with regard to the confessions to be studied. Nevertheless, the list is a good measure against which every preacher can assess his or her own theological training, and it is reproduced here for that purpose:

1. A survey course in the history of doctrine.
2. The ability to write a theological commentary on the Apostles' Creed, the Nicene Creed, and the Chalcedonian definition.
3. Knowledge of the development of the doctrine of the Trinity, culminating in the works of the Cappadocians and Augustine.
4. Reading and study of the following documents:
   The Letters of Ignatius.
   Justin's *Apology*.
   Athanasius' *The Incarnation of the Word*.
   Augustine's *The City of God*, and his *Confessions*.

Anselm's *Proslogium.*
Thomas Aquinas' *Summa Contra Gentiles,* chapters 1-25
or *Summa Theologica,* Q. 1-4.
Luther's writings of 1520: "Manifesto to the German
Nobility on the Improvement of the Christian Estate";
"On the Babylonian Captivity of the Church"; "The
Freedom of the Christian Man"; "Treatise on Good
Works."
Calvin's *The Institutes of the Christian Religion.*
Reformed confessions: The Geneva Catechism; The
Helvetic Confessions; The Scots Confession; The
Heidelberg Catechism, The Westminster Confession
of Faith and the Longer and Shorter Catechisms; The
Theological Declaration of Barmen.
Schleiermacher's *The Christian Faith.*
The systematic theology of either Turrettini, Charles
Hodge, A. A. Hodge, or H. L. J. Heppe.
Writings by Barth, Brunner, Otto Weber, and Rein-
hold Niebuhr.
5. The ability to explicate the following rubrics:
We believe in order to understand.
Faith seeks intelligibility.
Lex orandi, lex credendi.[9]

Those preachers who find their theological training
inadequate in the light of such a list can certainly begin to
compensate for their deficiences by reading and studying
on their own. Further, no preacher ever completes his or her
theological training in seminary. The process of understanding, appropriating, and using Bible and theological
tradition continues throughout one's ministry, and one's
knowledge and growth in Christian faith and practice
increase as one tries to live the Christian life in church and
society. The important point, however, is that it is almost
impossible ever to preach well, apart from a solid grounding
in Bible and church theology.

In the sermons that follow in this section, I have
tried to combine these three elements of preaching—
Scripture, church theology, art. All of the rhetorical devices

mentioned in this chapter can be found in these sermons, and perhaps the reader will pick out some of them. Because the originally oral sermons have been reduced to writing, many of their sounds and cadences and variations in timing have been muffled. Nevertheless, I have tried to set language at the service of the Word of God. The sermons use theology and Scripture in various ways, and these will be pointed out in the introductions to them, as guides to the reader's own methodology. In addition, after the initial doxological sermon, these messages are arranged in the order of the church year, and there are some brief discussions of the various liturgical seasons. The sermons are presented simply as illustrations of one preacher's attempts to fulfill this glorious calling to which we have been called—namely, to proclaim the Word of God faithfully, as stewards of his mysteries.

A. Doxology

The final purpose of all human life is to praise and honor God. As *The Shorter Catechism* puts it, "Man's chief end is to glorify God, and to enjoy him forever," and that glorification is to be rendered, not only in the act of worship, but also by our faithfulness and obedience to him in every area of our lives. The preacher needs to preach that purpose, because it gives meaning and worth to Christian life. The preacher, therefore, is confronted with the question, "How can I preach the praise of God?"

Certainly no passage of Scripture calls more insistently for praise of God than does Psalm 148. It is one of that collection of "Hallelujah Psalms," grouped together in Psalms 146-150 and so-called because they all begin and end in the Hebrew with *hallelu jah!* which means "Praise Yah!" (a shortened form of Yahweh), that is, "Praise the Lord!" In form, Psalm 148 is a hymn, with the introductory call to praise in vv. 1-13a, the transitional explanation for the praise, beginning with "for," in v. 13b, the body of the hymn in v. 14, and the concluding call to praise in v. 14d. Obviously, the introductory call to praise, stretching over thirteen verses, has been greatly expanded. This is a hymn that is insistent in its call to honor the Lord.

Two primary questions confronted me as I developed a sermon from this Psalm. First, how could I motivate the congregation to want to praise God? How could the "Hallelujah" of this Psalm become their heartfelt hallelujah? How could its words become their words? That is usually the approach that a preacher should take when using a Psalm text: to decide how to make the words of the Psalm become the words of his or her congregation. Some homileticians have felt that it is impossible to preach from the Psalms, because they view the Psalms solely as prayers of either praise or lament, and they do not think it possible to preach from a prayer. However, many of the Psalms are not prayers—as this one is not—and even those that are prayers can be used as texts for sermons, if the preacher will attempt to let the congregation identify with the words of the Psalm and make those words their own. So first, the problem of identifying with the words of the Psalm had to be dealt with.

Second and more difficult, this Psalm calls for praise not only from all human beings, but also from the total creation, animate and inanimate—while the ancient Hebrews had no difficulty with that, modern Americans do. How can you possibly talk, in any terms that make sense in our modern age, about the entire universe praising God? Obviously, any such presentation would have to be in highly metaphorical and poetical terms, because poetic language can get at truth that is otherwise inexpressible.

I solved this second hermeneutical problem of this Psalm when I read Lewis Thomas' *The Lives of a Cell*. There, in a brilliant essay on "The Music of *This* Sphere," Thomas portrays the sounds made by all creatures and things in the universe. Thomas' essay is totally secular, and he certainly draws different conclusions than do I in this sermon. But his language is marvelous, and his poetic view of his universe furnished me with the way to understand, in our scientific age, the universal call to praise in the Scripture lesson. The experience was a confirmation of my oft-repeated admonition to my students to read extensively in all types of literature.

The rest was easy: just follow the Scripture reading and its interpretive context in the whole of the canon. Because all the universe is called to praise, I introduced the sermon with the question about the purpose of creation as a whole, and moved naturally into Genesis 1:31's affirmation of the goodness of God's creation. The Scripture as a whole also has a good deal to say about the necessity of praise in human life, and this biblical theology was drawn upon and then used as a critique of the situation in our culture. Finally, the motivation for the congregation's praise could only be God's love in Jesus Christ which, according to the New Testament lesson, lies behind all creation: "all things were created through him and for him." But that love was spelled out in the sermon, not only in the usual terms of cross and resurrection, but also primarily in terms of God's work in and love for the natural world. That latter love was then contrasted with God's special love for humankind, made known to us in the teachings of Jesus. We must be careful in our proclamations not to dwell too exclusively on the cross, to the neglect of the other manifestations of God's love.

In the last point of the sermon, I returned closely to the Psalm, and joined together our praise with that given by God's universe, pointing out how its glorification of God supplements our own. Having been led thus far, the congregation was then asked to respond with praise and to make the words of the Psalm its own, and this was done by quoting portions of the Psalm at the end of the sermon. Such is always the function of a sermon's conclusion—to prompt the response from the congregation that the entire message has intended.

This sermon was first preached before a congregation of college students and professors in The First Presbyterian Church on the campus of Davidson College, North Carolina. We followed the sermon with the singing of St. Francis of Assisi's great hymn, "All Creatures of Our God and King."

Sample Sermon:

GOD THE MUSIC LOVER

Scripture: Psalm 148; Colossians 1:9-20

Let me ask you a weighty question. Why did God make the world? Karl Barth, the great Swiss theologian, once wrote, "The miracle is not that there is a God. The miracle is that there is a world." And that is true, for if you really stop to think about it, there is no reason whatsoever for the fact that God should have made this world. James Weldon Johnson imagined in his poem about the creation that God stepped out in space and said, "I'm lonely—I'll make me a world."[10] However, that conception, for all its beauty, not only ignores the fellowship of the Trinity but also embodies our perennial conceit: we seem to feel as if somehow God needed us petty human beings.

The truth is, of course, that he probably would have been a lot better off without us. We have given him nothing but trouble since he made us, and it shows the limitless patience of the Creator that he continues to bother with this world at all. Any lesser God would have washed his hands of the whole affair long ago.

And so the question remains, Why did God make the world? It is a question that philosophers and theologians have wrestled with for centuries: Why is there something? Why not nothing? Or as Annie Dillard put it in her prize-winning book: "The question from agnosticism is, Who turned on the lights? The question from faith is, Whatever for?"[11] Why did God make this world?

Now if I may engage in just a bit of whimsy this morning, I would like to suggest that God made this world and all that is in it because he is, first of all, a lover, but second, he made it because he is a music lover.

When we look about us at this universe in which we live, it is not difficult to believe that God made the world because he loves. We are surrounded on every side by works of extravagant beauty and variety and intricacy. The lowly housefly bears on his wings colors of breathtaking beauty,

62

as anyone knows who has ever looked through a microscope. The turtle drags along in the mud a belly plate marked with intricate pattern. The head of an ordinary caterpillar contains two hundred and twenty-eight separate and distinct muscles. And that's just speaking of very common creatures. What are we to say of wild flowers and scarlet tanagers and dogwood trees, of pink coral reefs and wooded hills and waterfalls, except that they are stamped with the love of a God wildly enthusiastic about his work? The author of Psalm 29 even looked at a thunderstorm, crashing out of the north to set woods afire and floods running and trees stripped of their leaves, and yet he proclaimed "Glory!" for the storm, too, speaks of the glory of a God, exuberant about his creation. I like Annie Dillard's phrase: "The Creator loves pizzazz!"[12] God loves his work. And so the author of Genesis 1 could say he pronounced it "very good." And Colossians could add, he made it through and for Jesus Christ. The love we have known in the Son of God is laid upon the world, and fashions out of the stuff of nothing the marvel of creation. God made the world through his Son, the Word, because he is a lover.

But he also made the world because he is a music lover. The answer to the love of God is to be the creation's echoing praise. The whole universe is to praise its Creator for the existence he has given it, for the good life he has made. In the Psalm that we read for our Old Testament lesson, there is a universal call to praise:

> Praise him sun and moon,
>   Praise him all stars of light . . .
> Fire and hail, snow and vapor,
>   stormy wind doing his word.
> The mountains and all hills,
>   trees of fruit and all cedars,
> Wild beasts and all cattle,
>   creeping things and winged fowl . . .
> Praise the name of the Lord
>   For he commanded and they were created.

So reads the ancient Hebrew. The response of the creation to its Creator is to be a thankful praise, a ringing hallelujah for the good life that God through his Son has made.

And God waits for that song of his creation to rise up to him, waits to hear the thankful affirmation, "Yes, life is very good," waits to hear the praise and know that all is right with his world. God is a music-lover, who wants to hear his creation sing, because when it sings he knows that his creation is as it should be, stamped with his love and overflowing with good, in a perfection of harmony.

All creation does try to sing a song of praise to its Maker. We think it is just poetic license and exaggeration when our Psalm talks about the universe singing and praising God, or when Job speaks of the morning stars singing together. But we do now know that there is a regular energy pulsing from quasars ten billion light years away, in a remarkable rhythm—that there is indeed a kind of music of the spheres.

I shall never forget a talk Leslie Newbigin gave one time about the nights he spent in the jungles of India. He said the dark was full of sounds—the roar of lions and shrieks of jackals and jabbering of monkeys. "And," asked Newbigin, "who hears all these things—there in the depths of the jungle of India night after night?" Well, God hears them. His creatures sing him songs in the night, and God loves the music and is very pleased that his creation is very good.

Ach, that's a bunch of nonsense, say our literalistic and pedantic minds. Maybe it is. But did you know that nature seems to abhor a silence, and that somewhere, underlying all the other signals, is a continual music? Lewis Thomas, the biologist, tells us, for example, that even lowly "termites make percussive sounds to each other by beating their heads against the floor in the dark, resonating corridors of their nests;" and spectrographic analysis of the sound "has recently revealed a high degree of organization in the drumming; the beats occur in regular, rhythmic phrases, differing in duration, like notes for a tympani section." Bats, as we all know, make sounds almost ceaselessly, to sense, by sonar, all the objects in their surroundings. But they have also been "heard to produce . . . strange, solitary, and lovely bell-like notes . . . while hanging at rest upside down in the depths of woods. . . . Fish make sounds by clicking their teeth, blowing air, and drumming with special muscles against tuned inflated air bladders."[13] Animals with loose skeletons rattle them. Even leeches tap rhythmically on leaves.

We know that humpback whales sing because recordings have been made of their songs, and we rational humans have concluded that their long, complex, insistent melodies are simply practical statements about navigation, or sources of food, or limits of territory. But how strange it seems that they should send "through several hundred miles of undersea such ordinary information as 'whale here.' " Sometimes, in the intervals between songs, they have been seen to breach and to leap clear of the waves, "landing on their backs, awash in the turbulence of their beating flippers."[14] It is as if they were showing sheer pleasure and jubilation for the way their song went, and yes, perhaps their praise for the joy of life.

Bird songs, of course, have been analyzed into nothing more than warning calls and mating messages and pronouncements of territory. But as Thomas puts it:

The thrush in my backyard sings down his nose in meditative, liquid runs of melody, over and over again, and I have the strangest impression that he does this for . . . pleasure. Some of the time he seems to be practicing, like a virtuoso in his apartment. He starts a run, reaches a midpoint in the second bar where there should be a set of complex harmonics, stops, and goes back to begin over, dissatisfied. Sometimes he changes his notation so conspicuously that he seems to be improvising sets of variations. It is a meditative . . . kind of music, and I cannot believe that he is simply saying, "thrush here."[15]

Yes, all creation praises its Maker. We only hear a few of the sounds at one time, but Thomas further suggests that if we could hear the combined sound that rises from the universe, it would lift us off our feet. But God hears it, and he is pleased. God is a music lover.

We human beings are supposed to join in the praise, of course. In the Psalm which we heard for our Old Testament lesson, not only nature is called to join the song, but also

> Kings of the earth and all peoples,
>   princes and all rulers of the earth,
> youths and also maidens,
>   old men and children.

Indeed, the Old Testament conception is that praise is synonymous with life. One of the chief characteristics of the dead in Hebrew thought was that they could not praise God, and that is one of the things that made the realm of Sheol, the place of the dead, so terrible. To live is to praise the Lord, according to the Bible, and if you do not praise, you are as good as dead.

Thus the biblical faith has always been a faith filled with the sound of song. From the song of Miriam at the time of the exodus through the songs of the Psalter, to the hymn at the Last Supper and the singing of Paul and Silas in prison and finally the pictured hallelujah chorus in the Kingdom of God in Revelation, those who trust are those who sing songs of praises to God, the music lover. It is the chief end of man, says the Westminster Confession, to glorify God and enjoy him forever. Or in our New Testament lesson, all things were created for Christ. We were made to praise his name, along with all creation, in songs of praise and thanksgiving.

The difficulty is that we have interrupted the praise. We have interrupted it with the still, sad song of humanity. Think what we have done to the song of praise our Old Testament lesson called for from the old men and children. The song of the old man is now the mumbling stupor of the resident of a nursing home—in pain, alone, forgotten, and drugged to keep him quiet until he dies. The song of the child has become the whimpering cry of millions of hungry infants in Cambodia and India and famine-ridden parts of Africa, or conversely it has become the scornful laugh of irresponsibility on the lips of the over-gratified younster in America.

Or think what we have done to the song of praise from grizzly bear and coyote, from whale and sea lion, and eagle and whooping crane—all those endangered species. We are slaughtering off the sound of their singing. Indeed, we human beings have ravished the world with our bug sprays and poisons and technology, with our bulldozers and concrete and earth-movers, and now the day seems not far distant when God the music lover will listen and hear from his good earth nothing but a deafening silence.

It is profound the way the prophets of the Old Testament picture the end of the world. Jeremiah talks about the time when there shall no longer be the sound of mirth and of singing, when no voice of feasting or merriment will interrupt the stillness caused by sin. His last apocalyptic picture of judgment is a picture of awful silence, when there is no bird left to sing on a bush and no man and no light. It is a picture that could very well portray our world after the final hydrogen bomb is dropped. The earth is left a still, dark sphere, turning silently in space, with no sound but the whistling of that stormy wind, blowing once again over the void of chaos. Has our sin become the vast acoustical tile by which we are slowly but surely walling in the universe and creating for ourselves that ghostly and ghastly stillness? "This is the way the world ends/Not with a bang but a whimper."[16] Silence—because we are destroying the song of praise.

I know of no way to restore the song, except that one given in both our Scripture readings—to become lovers of God, because we see the love with which he has first loved us.

> Praise the name of Yahweh (reads our Psalm)
>   For exalted is his name alone.
> His majesty is over the earth and heavens
>   and he has raised up a horn (i.e., salvation) for his people.
> Praise is for all his saints,
>   for the children of Israel, a people near to him.

You see, we have systematically failed to praise God for the life he has given us, and we have systematically and wantonly destroyed his good earth. But God will not have done with us! There is the final miracle—that he will not rest content with our sin and silence. He will not deliver us into the dominion of darkness and its stillness unto death.

Instead, he has sent his own Son into our wasting and wasted lives, to walk this world with us, and he has said, Here, here is the measure of my love for you; here is my forgiveness of your sin. You have laid waste my world and ignored my love, stamped on earth and sea and heavens. But you are more important to me than my sparrows, than the grass which clothes my meadows. You are of infinitely more worth than my lilies in the field.

Do you remember Jesus' teaching when he told those things to us? "Look at the birds of the air," he said. "Are you not of more value than they?" And "consider the lilies of the field, how they grow; they neither toil nor spin; yet I tell you, even Solomon in all his glory was not arrayed like one of these. But if God so clothes the grass of the field, which today is alive and tomorrow is thrown into the oven, will he not much more clothe you, O [ye] of little faith?"

God loves us even more than he loves his beloved creation. That is a fantastic thought. God loves you more than all the wonders of his world. Think of the care he lavishes on the birds—clothing them in gorgeous colors, providing them trees for nests and infinite melodies in song, guiding their instincts year by year in their seasonal migrations, feeding them with bug and berry and giving them drink from the rain. And yet Jesus says, "Are you not of more value than they?" God lavishes on you more care and love in his Son Jesus Christ than he has lavished on all his creation through him. And so the profound and familiar hymn can sing it:

> Fair are the meadows,
> Fairer still the woodlands,
> Robed in the blooming garb of spring;
> Jesus is fairer, Jesus is purer,
> Who makes the woeful heart to sing.

God loves you more than he loves all creation. And so he gives his very Son for you on a cross to restore to you abundant life, that you may have joy and hope and learn once again how it is to sing. And Christ is raised from the dead that you may truly have the power to love your neighbor, that old man and that woman and that child to whom we are to minister. Is there any one of us here so sunk into sinful and sullen silence that we cannot, that we will not, praise God for such love?

But then, good Christian saints, is our feeble praise sufficient to laud the love of such a God? Or do we not, with our Psalmist, need to be joined in our praise by a universal chorus? When our voices are feeble in their song to God, do we not need the mighty whale's jubilation? When we sleep tonight, do we not need the night creatures' roars and shrieks of joy—the endangered tiger, the wolf, the Rocky Mountain grizzly? When we are inconstant, should there not be the steady pulsation of the distant stars, beaming their energy through an unpolluted sky? And when we are dissonant and divided in our praise, should not our disharmony be drowned out by the liquid melodies of lark and wren, or the roar of pure waterfalls?

Our Scripture lesson from Colossians proclaims that all things hold together in Christ. And perhaps this is finally the way we affirm that that is really true—by so loving our God in his Son that we will not disrupt the song of one old man or child, that we will not still a single sparrow's song raised to him in praise, or pollute the waters of one fish that bubbles out its joy, or condone setting out a trap of poison for one coyote howling his hallelujah. Then indeed God's universe can be joined together as one, sounding forth its great, unbroken Te Deum in one united chorus of praise, for the love that God has lavished upon us in his Son. And God, the music lover, can hear and smile and rejoice over his work, and affirm once again, as he did at the beginning, "Behold, it is very good."

And so, good Christians, praise the Lord!

Praise the Lord from the earth . . .
Mountains and all hills,
    fruit trees and all cedars!
Beasts and all cattle,
    creeping things and flying birds!

69

You young men and maidens together,
  you old men and children!
Praise the name of the Lord,
  for his name alone is exalted,
  his glory is above earth and heaven.
He has raised up salvation for his people;
  Praise is for all of you, his saints;
for you are the people who are near to him.
Therefore, praise the Lord! Praise the Lord!
Hallelu-jah!

                                                            Amen.

B. Preaching for Advent/Christmas

In contrast with the previous sermon, the following Advent sermon is totally controlled by one Scripture lesson. The boundaries of the appointed lesson for the day have been expanded from Luke 3:1-6, to include the thoughts extending through verse 18. But the theme for the second Sunday in Advent in Cycle C has been retained, namely, the theme of repentance.

It is not an easy theme to preach on. Modern congregations often have no sense of sinfulness and therefore cannot be brought to repentance. As a talk-show host once said to Billy Graham on TV, "I don't know what sin is anymore." In our modern, anything-goes society, many of our parishioners share the same ignorance. The preacher therefore has the task of first convicting the people of their sin, before talking about repentance. John the Baptist's preaching is perfect for the task. Step-by-step, the Baptist lays out God's demands upon us, and the preacher need only rephrase those demands in terms of modern life, as does this sermon.

Before that is done in this message, however, there is careful attention given to a description of the historical figure of the Baptist and to the meaning of his appearance in the Gospel according to Luke—all of which can be gleaned from the commentaries. John the Baptist is announcing the coming of the kingdom of God to his hearers, and the sermon makes the meaning of that kingdom clear by spelling out its content in terms of Old Testament prophecy. In short, though his sermon is controlled by the Lucan lesson, the figure of John is set in the content of the biblical *Heilsgeschichte* or sacred history.

The sermon then moves to a section designed to make the congregation *want* the kingdom to come. So often we announce the good news to our congregations without first showing them that they need it and without motivating them to desire it! The American way of life is so comfortable that most of our people, if they were truthful, would say that they want the kingdom of God to come—but not yet. Life is too good as it is, and our people have no desire to hurry on past it to the kingdom. The preacher has to remind the congregation of its public and private hurts and longings and make them want the kingdom's healings with all their hearts. The excerpt from the United Nations Charter is simply one illustration quoted for that purpose.

The sermon moves on: if we want the kingdom of God that comes in the child of Bethlehem, how can we get to his manger? Here, John's demands for repentance that bears fruit are spelled out in detail. Repentance is seen not simply as a feeling, but as a transformation of one's actions. The preacher needs always to define theological terms such as "repentance," and the Baptist's preaching is perfectly suited to the task. So often the Scripture lesson itself will define theological terms for us, and we have only to follow its lead.

We have now arrived at a point in the sermon where we see that we are totally captive to sin and that we cannot fulfill the demands of God as they have been preached to us by the Baptist. The sermon therefore moves into the announcement of the good news that we have a Savior, despite our captivity to sin and despite our inability to bear fruit that befits repentance: in some ways, this sermon more purely announces grace than does any other sermon in this volume.

One particular point should be noted, however: all of the descriptions of Jesus are taken from the Gospel according to Luke. None are drawn from the other synoptics or from the Fourth Gospel. When preaching from a gospel pericope, the preacher should use only that particular gospel's portrayal of our Lord, and not try to harmonize or homogenize it with the portrayal given by the other evangelists.

At the end, the sermon returns to the theme of repentance and defines it in terms of all that has been said, thus holding the whole together around its one theme. But the gospel's glad news is reaffirmed in the final sentence.

This sermon was first preached before a seminary congregation during a Sunday evening worship service in Watts Chapel on the campus of Union Theological Seminary in Richmond. It is addressed to a congregation of believing and practicing Christians, and it had the task of calling them to the repentance that is an integral part of the Christian life.

Sample Sermon:

OF REPENTANCE AND CAPTIVITY

Scripture: Luke 3:1-18

In order to get to Bethlehem, we have to get past John the Baptist. So the church, in its long experience with the Christian life, has decided. This is the Second Sunday in Advent, the third year in the three-year lectionary cycle, and the first six verses of the lesson, which we heard from the Gospel according to Luke, are the appointed reading for the day. By choosing this lesson, the church is saying that if we really want to go to Bethlehem's manger, then first we should meet the Baptist, and that is not a comfortable prospect at all.

It is not accidental that we do not often include the Baptist in our Christmas celebrations. He is a very unsettling figure, there at work in the Judean wilderness, interrupting his preaching only long enough for a lunch of locusts and wild honey. He is clothed in camel's hair and sweats under the desert sun—beard and hair streaked with dust, feet in sandals caked with mud. He reeks of poverty and a wild zeal and some rock-hard discipline. He is not a character you work up in ceramics and place beside the sweet cherubs and lambs round the creche. He does not go with shepherds and angels and peace on earth, good will toward men.

And yet everyone of the Gospel writers has him there toward the beginning. They cannot tell the story of Jesus without him. So perhaps just this once we need to accept the church's discipline and confront John the Baptist, in order that we may fully know how to receive the child wrapped in swaddling cloths and laid in a manger.

When we admit the Baptist onto our Advent stage, it becomes very clear, first of all, that there is something decisive afoot. John is not meant to be Elijah, the messianic forerunner, in Luke's Gospel. But neither is he a casual circuit rider, who comes around once a year to preach. No, when John appears, the kingdom of God is at hand. There is no more business as usual if we let John on the scene, no more standard routines and lists checked off as you have always done it: shopping, Christmas cards, baking, wrapping presents, church rehearsals and programs— there, that's it for another year! No, we are dealing with eternity now, with John on the scene.

The time has filled up. Prophetic vision has piled on top of prophetic vision, until there is no more room. There are visions of a renewed people and of their righteous king, visions of the stony hearts taken out of us and replaced with obedient hearts of flesh, visions of the Spirit poured out and the glory of the Lord revealed, visions of everlasting peace with God and of a new and eternal covenant—of living water for those who thirst and of wine and milk without price. Time has filled up with a surfeit of visions, until there is no more room, and now they are all about to spill out into history and become the stuff of your life and mine. The kingdom of God is at hand. "Affairs are now soul-size."

> The frozen misery
> Of centuries breaks, cracks, begins to move.[17]

The whole creation has groaned and travailed in its sin through the weight of interminable years. Now God stands at the door and is about to break in with a new creation.

"Prepare the way of the Lord!" John cries. We have to do with the final time now this Christmas, when every decision we make and every act we do will be decisive for our eternity. "Even now the ax is laid to the root of the trees," proclaims John. "Every tree therefore that does not bear good fruit is cut down and thrown into the fire." With the Baptist on the scene it cannot be Christmas as usual.

And yet, for all the burning necessity for decision that John brings with him at this season, it is also a hopeful sign that he has now appeared, is it not? We very much need the coming of the kingdom of God that John announces. Our lives are so full of our public and private hurts, so weary from their constant fight with evil. It would indeed be good tidings of a great joy to hear that God is coming with his salvation—his release from it all and his renewal. No wonder multitudes went out to hear him when John appeared with that message.

In a book I was reading the other day, I chanced to come across an excerpt from the preamble to the United Nations Charter, first published in June of 1945. And I was struck by how ironic the words of that preamble sound in 1984. Listen to what they say:

We, the peoples of the United Nations, determined to save succeeding generations from the scourge of war, which twice in our lifetime has brought untold sorrow to mankind, and to reaffirm faith in fundamental human rights, in the dignity and worth of the human person, in the equal right of men and women and of nations large and small . . .
And for these ends to practice tolerance and live together in peace with one another as good neighbors . . .
Have resolved to combine these efforts to accomplish our aims.

How hollow and empty of its promise that magnificent dream now appears! Yes, we could use the healing in the kingdom of God that John announces. He promises that all flesh shall see the Lord's salvation. We very much need to go to Bethlehem this year to receive it.

But to get to Bethlehem, we first must be done with John the Baptist; and John there in the wilderness, with his wild-eyed zeal and his rock-hard discipline, lays some requirements upon us. For Luke, John is the last and the greatest of the prophets, and like all the prophets, he announces some conditions for entering the kingdom. He comes to us, as he came to his compatriots, preaching a baptism of repentance for the forgiveness of sins. John's requirement for receiving the Lord's salvation this Christmas is that we repent of our wrong.

Well, that does not seem so difficult. In fact it is a requirement that we are well on the way to fulfilling. We know that Advent is the season of repentance and preparation for the coming of the Christ child. We know that God loves the humble, the meek, the poor in spirit, the confessing sinner. And so we gladly acknowledge our wrong in prayers of confession, Sunday after Sunday— maybe not in too many specifics, to be sure, but certainly in general. We gladly pay lip-service to the theological truth that we are all miserable sinners and that somehow, though we are not quite sure how, all our thoughts and actions are tainted with Adam's fall. We are good biblical Christians after all, and our general sinfulness is a part of our creed. And so with downcast eyes and humble mien and a "mea culpa" on our lips, we think to hurry on past John the Baptist on our way to the manger in Bethlehem.

But the Baptist blocks our way, with a pointing finger and a fierce, harsh cry: "You brood of vipers! Who warned you to flee from the wrath to come? Bear fruits that befit repentance!" Our piety is not enough, you see. We cannot just confess our sins. The confession has to bear fruit in hearts transformed and in lives changed from the inside out. "I'm sorry" has to issue in wrong righted in our neighborhoods and responsibilities accepted, in grudges forgotten and disputes healed between husband and wife, or parent and child. "I repent" has to bring forth deeds of simple justice in our society and not-so-simple love—the weak protected, the oppressed freed, the helpless supported and succored. "Be ye therefore perfect, even as your Father which is in heaven is perfect!" (KJV)—John brings to mind that command, John there with his burning word and his rock-hard discipline. And you and I cannot get past that Baptist, for all our pleas of repentance, because our pious confessions of sin have not born their fruits of righteous living. As a Jew once put it succinctly, "You are Christians. That is why I am a Jew."

So John forms a barrier there on our way to Bethlehem, because John demands that we live lives of righteousness and justice and truth. That is the only way, he proclaims, that you and I will get into the kingdom with its salvation.

Shall we try another approach, then, to get past this troublesome figure? We very much need the healing of God. We have simply got to share in the kingdom's coming. We must be there when the Dayspring from on high comes down to give light to those who sit in darkness and in the shadow of death—when he comes to guide our feet into the way of his peace. We must be there at Christmas. And so if we cannot rely on our own righteousness, perhaps we can get by on the merit of others. We are children of Abraham, let's say, or of Calvin, or of Wesley, or of Luther. We are members of the covenant people, the chosen ones of God. We are the church, for God's sake, John! We belong at Bethlehem. In fact, we are the very ones who prepare the way of the Lord for all the other people. We are the ones who welcome the Lord, who show him forth to the rest of the world; we are the ones who bear witness to his mighty deeds. Surely this heritage in which we share qualifies us to be at the manger. Surely the Lord would not shut out from the kingdom all of us who are Christians! That would be ridiculous, like cutting off his nose to spite his face.

But the word that comes back at us from John is that he excommunicates us all. God "has scattered the proud in the imagination of their hearts," just as Mary said he would. For John's reply is once more, "You brood of vipers! Do not try to stand on your religious privileges. You are not all that indispensable to the Lord. He could raise up sons of Abraham—or children of Calvin or Wesley or Luther—for himself from the very stones."

Let us stop kidding ourselves. We do not prepare the way of the Lord. Usually we just manage to place obstacles in his way instead. We are so concerned for our own status, our own tradition, our own way of doing things, that we shut out from our church and our esteem all who do not agree with us—you know, all those high-church Anglicans and low-church Baptists and above all, the fundamentalists. Do you really think that all we have done in the past few years in our various denominational headquarters has prepared the way of the Lord? Very often we become stumbling blocks to the acceptance of the gospel. And our pride in our religious heritage or our manipulations of the church's life become precisely the crooked ways that God has to straighten out. Well, straighten us out he does through this Baptist, the last of his prophets. "You have no claim on the Lord," John tells us. "God could raise up the very stones to take your place if he had to. You have no reserved box to watch the beginning of the kingdom at Bethlehem."

So the new age, the fullness of time, the completion of all the prophets' promises, will begin to take place in the city of David, and we have no way to be there. Our sins of unrighteousness and pride have barred us from the manger. The way there is indeed narrow and those who will be saved will be few. The householder has risen up and shut the door, and we stand still on the outside.

The paradox of all this is that Luke says that this is good news that John is preaching. Verse 18 of our Scripture lesson reads, "So, with many other exhortations, he preached good news to the people." Have we missed something somewhere? How can what we have heard possibly be good news? John has announced to us in effect that there really is no way this year we can have a merry Christmas. "Behold I bring you good tidings of great joy?" Forget it! We know now that the proper translation of the rest of the passage is "Peace on earth, good will among men with whom he is pleased." And God, the Baptist has made us realize, is not pleased with us sinful church members. When we ask in dismay, as did John's contemporaries, "What then shall we do?" the answer comes back in those uncompromising tones that belonged to all Israel's prophets:

"You rich and comfortable, share what you have with

those who are hungry and ill clad!" Ah yes, we remember now. We have hunger and poverty crises in our world, and give as we may and try as we may, we really have not made a dent in them. In fact, we have the uneasy feeling that we may never end them. We find ourselves helpless before the magnitude and complexity of the problems.

But John says more: "You tax collectors"—or let's put it in terms of us—"you subversives, you traitors in the kingdom of God, stop undermining the rule of God with your selfishness and self-seeking." And that's just the trouble with you and me—we can't get rid of ourselves. Reinhold Niebuhr, who probably understood our self-seeking better than any other theologian, once characterized it this way:

One of the hazards about the [Christian life] is that the more successful you are [at it], the more you will be subject to various temptations of pride and exhibitionism. I give myself in one moment to a cause of the word of our Lord, and then I discover in the next moment that I have not given myself at all, but that the self stands outside in this process of self-giving and asks, "Does anybody notice me in my virtues, or will they give proper credit for it?[18]

Yes, that's the trouble we have with your words, John the Baptist—we cannot get rid of ourselves.

But there is still another command: "You persons who exercise power and authority, temper your power with justice." That really makes us know we are lost, because we are participants in a powerful and unjust society. Daily you and I take part in a multitude of unjust power-plays. Ours are the taxes that support CIA assassinations and courts that favor the rich. Ours are the votes behind a welfare system that encourages the breakup of families. Ours are the voices that are silent in the face of media violence and profitable pornography and immorality in high and low places. Daily you and I, through our society, trample the poor and pervert our young and give our sanction to slavery to evil. And we feel utterly powerless to change ourselves and our city, much less our entire country. Our world has gone mad—power-hungry and wealth-thirsty—and we are carried along in its dash toward destruction, helpless to halt its insane rush toward the lower reaches of hell.

We are captives, you and I, captives to the power of sin. And because we do not and cannot fulfill the demands that John the Baptist lays upon us, it is quite clear that we cannot have a place in the kingdom of God—that kingdom that begins at Christmastime in the child of Bethlehem. John supposedly announced good news, but it is not good to us. It is instead the announcement of our certain condemnation.

And yet, I wonder. I wonder if John's good news consisted not so much in what he was announcing as in whom he was pointing to. And I even wonder if the Baptist fully realized the nature of the Mighty One who was coming after him, the thong of whose sandals he said he was not worthy to untie. John pictured the coming Messiah with his winnowing fork in his hand, ready to clear his threshing floor and to gather the wheat into his granary; and when he announces that, we have the sinking and certain feeling that we are just going to get left in the heap with the chaff, instead of being gathered into the barn.

But instead of that Lord of judgment, who certainly would condemn you and me, John found on his hands, according to Luke, a good shepherd of a hundred sheep, looking for the one that was lost—the teller of a tale about a father running down the road to welcome a prodigal son—a friend of outcasts and sinners and those who broke all the rules. John found himself confronted by a king who acted more like a servant, and so puzzled was he by the figure of Jesus that he had to send a messenger to ask, "Are you he who is to come, or shall we look for another?" Are you indeed the beginning and content of the righteous kingdom of God?

Jesus was and is the one. With his birth at Bethlehem, God broke into our very real world in final victory. He came into the world of Tiberius Caesar and our world of unjust power politics. He came into the realm of a Caiaphas and our realm of phony piety. He came into a world suffering under the haughtiness of a Herod and under our selfishness. But he came, not as an avenging conqueror, his winnowing fork in his hand, but as a humble man of Nazareth, who stood up in his hometown synagogue on a sabbath day and read a passage about a servant, to characterize his ministry.

> The Spirit of the Lord is upon me,
>   because he has anointed me to preach
>   good news to the poor.
> He has sent me to proclaim release to
>   the captives
>   and recovering of sight to the blind.

Good Christians, could it be that we, weighed down with our burden of wealth and things, are nevertheless those poor, because we are dressed in tattered rags of righteousness, without a scrap of justification to call our own? Rich by the standards of this world, we are poor beggars when it comes to goodness. Could it be, too, that we are those captives of whom Christ spoke, unable to free ourselves from our sin, who despite all our struggles to do the right thing usually end up doing wrong? What a mess we make of our world and of our lives and of the lives of our loved ones, despite all our good intentions! How imprisoned we are in our selfishness and pride and terrible, terrible blindness!

And you see, it is precisely to us—as those poor, those captives, those blind—that Christ comes this Christmas season, bearing with him his forgiveness and his release from guilt and his Spirit which will empower us. It is precisely to us, who are imprisoned in this world of unjust power and selfishness and evil, who never seem able to break free to do the right, who therefore have not a ghost of a chance of deserving to be at Bethlehem—precisely to us, us captives, to all captives, the good news is announced that we nevertheless have a Savior. Gerard Manley Hopkins once said it:

> I say that we are wound
> with mercy round and round
> as if with air.[19]

We are surrounded by mercy—mercy that receives us as beloved children into the presence and realm of God our Father, mercy that pours its Spirit into our hearts until sin's power over us is broken, mercy that makes us its servants of love and justice and goodness in this world—this world which, in fact, is becoming the kingdom of our Lord and of his Christ. We have a Savior, good Christians, a Savior who comes at this Christmastime, precisely because you and I desperately need to be saved.

And so our repentance in this Advent season is not the offering of our own righteousness to God. John the Baptist has made us know that we have none whatsoever to offer. No, our repentance is our emptiness—our empty hands and empty hearts—and our reaching out for the saving hand of the Mighty One who comes in that child of Bethlehem. Our repentance in this Advent season is our waiting, our waiting in our captivity for the arrival of the One who can free us. Our repentance is our eager longing for the appearance of our Savior. And he comes, friends—oh yes, he comes!

Amen.

C. Preaching for Epiphany

The following sermon's Scripture lesson, John 14:1-12, is actually the stated lesson for Eastertide 5A in the ecumenical lectionary, and the sermon in fact was preached on that particular Sunday. But I have set it here under an Epiphany heading, because Epiphany deals with the manifestation or revelation of Christ to the Gentile world, and that certainly was the purpose of this sermon. It was first preached in the Memorial Church of Harvard University—a church that has a group of faithful Christians who worship there regularly, but a church that also is frequented by many visitors to the campus, by casual onlookers who have come to hear the magnificent choir, and by those who have no faith or interest in Jesus Christ whatsoever. In recent years, a number of followers of Sun Myung Moon have also attended Harvard Divinity School, and Harvard has that syncretistic atmosphere common to the student body of any large university. The sermon therefore shares the purpose of the Epiphany season.

In developing this sermon, I purposely substituted the reading from Exodus 33 for the other two stated lessons. I always highly recommend to homiletics students that they begin their preaching ministries by following the lectionary for two or three years. Such practice forces them to deal with a stated text, rather than with a sermon idea, and they gain expertise in preaching from the Bible, while avoiding concentration on their own pet themes. They also educate their congregations in the glories of the church year, which sets the congregations' lives into the framework of the life of Christ. But after that initiation into lectionary preaching, I recommend to students that they use the lectionary with flexibility, especially in regard to the Old Testament. Large and important sections of the Old Testament, which should be used by the pulpit, are omitted from the lections, and usually the Old Testament is viewed in the lectionary only as prophecy of Christ's coming. There is, therefore, a rather narrow view of the Old Covenant's content built into the stated lessons, and I like to enlarge on that view frequently.

In this sermon, however, the Old Testament lesson from Exodus 33:12-18 is used simply because it shares a common motif with John 14:1-11 and can serve, therefore, to enrich the language of the sermon. With its concluding verses 19-23, it really deserves sermonic treatment in its own right, because it is a magnificent passage. But most of the content of this particular sermon was taken from the Gospel according to John and specifically from the stated lesson of John 14.

Some preachers who read this sermon may think to themselves that they have done a much more complete job in their own preaching in explicating the meaning of Jesus as "the way, the truth, and the life"—a famous text. But in assessing those explications, they should ask themselves if they have actually preached the meaning of those terms as the Fourth Gospel understands them, or have they brought in outside ideas and imposed them on the text? The Gospel according to John has its own peculiar theology, which is distinctively different from the theology found in the Synoptic Gospels. John is concerned about the nature of reality—about the nature of God—and about the person of Jesus as the sole revealer of that reality. It is in that context that Jesus must be described as "the way, the truth, and the life," and this sermon so describes him.

The portrayal of Jesus in the sermon is taken solely from the Fourth Gospel and is not harmonized with the Synoptics' witness (see the preface to the previous sermon). Were such harmonization attempted, I would have ended with a picture of Jesus not found in any portion of the New Testament and, therefore, with a picture not true to the biblical witness.

Because the sermon was directed not only to a Christian congregation, but also to the doubters, the waverers, the syncretists, and the casual visitors in its midst, it starts out with the recognition of religion as a universal human phenomenon—a concession to the fact that one sometimes has to lead unbelievers rather gently into a confrontation with the Christian faith. The sermon also tries to tie into universal human hungers—specifically, the hungers for meaning in the face of death and for comfort and guidance in the midst of trouble. As in the previous sermons, those notes are designed to arouse desire for the good news of Christ.

The sermon then explores some of the substitutes that our culture has found in its quest for God, drawing on specific idolatries of our time: secularism, eastern mysticism, Moonism, the cult of self-fulfillment. Such sustitutes for God appear with the times, and the preacher always has to be aware of what particular idol his or her congregation has erected at the foot of its own Sinai.

The last portion of the sermon moves away from apologetics, however, into witness and proclamation, and the reason for that is clear: no person, in any congregation, can be argued into believing the Christian faith, no matter how persuasive the preacher or how desperate the listener's need. Christian faith is born simply by hearing the gospel:

"Faith comes from what is heard, and what is heard comes by the preaching of Christ." Faith is a gift born out of the work of the Holy Spirit in our listeners' hearts. We preachers therefore finally have the task of preaching Christ, and that is what this sermon tries to do in its last section—to testify to Jesus Christ. The sermon has tried to prepare the congregation to receive him, has tried to show them their need of him and has testified to his humility, obedience, and love that so outshine the darkness of all our idols. But then the sermon, in its methodology, does what its conclusion calls the congregation to do: it trusts Christ. It trusts his Father and the working of Christ's Spirit to bring home to the lives of the congregation the truth of the gospel. Beyond that trust, we preachers cannot and must not try to go. Our people are not saved by our works, any more than they are saved by their own. They are saved by God, who works in their ears and minds and wills and hearts through his Spirit, to bring them to faith in his saving action. We plant, we water, but God gives the growth. So we believe, and so we preach.

Sample Sermon:

ON LIVING IN REALITY

Scripture: Exodus 33:12-18
John 14:1-11

We stand on the shores of this world's mysteries, and gaze longingly out over their depths. For all of our learning and science—indeed, perhaps because of them—we know how much we do not know. What really causes cancer cells to run amok? How does the human brain work, and what triggers its impulses? Do electrons circle their nuclei wholly by chance, and if so, what holds this universe together? Even our language is an enigma to us: Is it necessary for thought? Or just what is the human personality and what happens to it after death? On every shore of learning, the waters of mystery lap at our feet, and out there in the mists dwell the creatures of the strange and the unknown. Some ancient map makers used to mark the unexplored regions of their world with the phrase, "Here be dragons." We could mark the limits of our understanding with the words, "Here be mystery."

Biologist Lewis Thomas, who is head of the Sloan-Kettering Institute, once made the marvelous suggestion that we should all agree not to push the atomic bomb button until we have completely understood just one form of life on earth. He then proceeded to demonstrate that we do not fully understand the lowest protozoa. If Thomas' suggestion were made a universal law and applied to our understanding of ourselves, we would never blow up our world, for beyond all the other mysteries, we do not understand ourselves and our hunger for God.

What is it about the human race that has led it in every culture and clime to construct some form of religion? To presuppose some one or some thing beyond itself? Heaven knows, we human beings think of ourselves most of the time as quite self–sufficient, or at least sufficient in relation to just one other person—even Robinson Crusoe had to have his man Friday. But in the deepest depths of our self-centered wisdom, we know there is someone else out there. Behind the mists of the mysteries of this world, there is a greater mystery still. Perhaps someone watching. Perhaps some good to which we are responsible. Perhaps some source in which we dimly sense we have our origin and being and, therefore, someone or something to which we know we have to answer.

In T. S. Eliot's play, *The Cocktail Party,* Celia talks of her strange sense of responsibility: "It's not the feeling of anything I've ever done," she says, "which I might get away from, or of anything in me I could get rid of—but of emptiness, of failure toward someone, or something, outside of myself; And I feel I must—atone."[20] And when some callous criminal lacks that sense of responsibility, we call him an animal, and we want to lock him up in a cage for a lack of remorse. To be human, it would almost seem, is to have some sense of God, and we hunger after searching out the depths of that mystery too.

Especially do we hunger to search out God when we face the question of meaning. The days wear on. The years progress. Our life's labors and loves trickle out and cease. And we look back on the stream of the years and wonder after their purpose. Did they flow into some broader current and contribute to some wider meaning, which will finally find its ocean flow in the greater depths of a divine and goodly purpose? Or is our little trickle of life cut off from all other meaning, and destined simply to disappear in the sands of time and evil?

Philip asked that question, according to our New Testament lesson, when that little band of eleven remaining disciples huddled about their leader. Jesus shortly was going to die. Death stood just outside the door. And Philip needed reassurance about the meaning of it all. "Lord, show us the Father," he begged of Jesus, "and it will be enough for us." Beyond us, beyond the evil out there on the city streets, beyond the power and pettiness of humankind, that will soon kill the fairest life we have ever known on this earth, "Lord, show us the Father, and it will be enough." Show us that beyond our years, God remains and is at work. Show us that your cross will not crucify him too. Show us that though death comes, there is still a good purpose for living. As we grow old and our own death approaches, we hunger for God and meaning.

We also hunger to search him out when we need comfort and guidance. A relationship we have known with some person we love crumbles and turns to dust, and we find ourselves in a desert of loneliness or regret. A crucial decision hangs heavy on our heart, and we do not know which way to turn, because either way seems nothing but a wilderness of complication and risk. Anxiety or pain or dread of future possibility turns our mouths dry with the taste of fear, and we thirst for some release, some certain direction, some covering love. And so like Moses in our Old Testament lesson, with a rebellious and fearful people on his hands, and nothing ahead but desert and danger and dry unknown, we long for a protecting presence to forgive, and to go with us, and to guide us. "Lord, I pray thee," becomes our prayer, "show me thy glory." Show me thy love that can overcome all my broken human relationships. Show me thy guiding hand that can point out the way. Show me thy might that can defeat the dangers of this world's wilderness. Lord, show us the Father and it will be enough for us.

Well, what do you get back when you cry out for God, when you probe the deepest mystery that human life has to offer—indeed, when you pass beyond all mysteries and knowledge to search for the Wholly Other? *Ens realissimum*, the medieval philosophers called him—the most real Being there is. What do you find when you search out that most real Reality? Nothing? Does your cry of "Father! Father! Father!" simply die out in the echoes of empty space, and do you therefore conclude with the character in John Osborne's play that "We're alone in the universe, there's no God, it just seems that it all began by something as simple as sunlight striking a piece of rock. And here we are. We've only got ourselves. Somehow, we've just got to make a go of it.[21]

Or do you end up with a caricature of a god, a ridiculous little human being, who calls himself a new messiah, as his tongue struts through the earth—a new Hitler like Jim Jones, a mystic guru, a self-proclaimed savior, a Korean Sun Myung Moon? Or perhaps does the face of the god we seek turn out only to be our own, and we find that the most real thing in our lives is our own self-fulfillment or selfish gratification?

What do you find when you search out God? Robert Oppenheimer told of watching the mushroom cloud of the first atomic bomb explosion at Los Alamos and thinking to himself of the Hindu god of destruction. "Now is Shiva let loose," he whispered—Shiva, with his serpent and his necklace of skulls—a three-eyed monster of death: a dumb, dark, dreaming thing that turns the handle of this evil show. Is that what is really real in this world of ours? Death, destruction, evil, suffering? And so should we, with Shiva's followers, deny that there is any goodness and any meaning in human history and seek ascetic absorption into Brahma?

What do you find when you search out God? Illusion, pride, selfishness, death? If those are the really real in our world, then may we be delivered from their evil. If those are gods, then better we should all be atheists.

"Lord, show us the Father, and it will be enough for us." And Jesus replied to him, "Have I been with you so long, and yet you do not know me, Philip? He who has seen me has seen the Father . . . I am in the Father and the Father in me . . . the Father who dwells in me does his works." If we search out God through the pages of the New Testament, if we ask what its writers found supremely real, then we are presented with a series of pictures that portray a different sort of God.

He comes to us in the flesh and blood of a human being, to be sure—the Ultimate Mystery of the universe reveals himself by way of Bethlehem and Nazareth. But unlike our self-proclaimed messiahs, he comes in deepest humility—a master, with a towel at his waist, down on one knee, with a basin of water, washing the dust from the calluses of Peter's feet, and Philip's, and yes, even of Judas'. He claims nothing for himself: "My glory is nothing," he says; "the Son can do nothing of his own accord"; "I do not speak on my own authority." And that costs him the crown of thorns and the mockery, the scourging, the thirst, and the nails—and finally the thrust of the spear in his side, and his life-juices emptied out. Pride and selfishness bow before the humility and obedience of Jesus of Nazareth.

And evil bows before his love. "Having loved his own who were in the world, he loved them to the end," the gospel tells us. And so we see him here in our New Testament lesson, reassuring his disciples before he goes out to die, preparing them for his crucifixion and departure out of this world. "Let not your hearts be troubled, neither let them be afraid." "I will not leave you desolate; I will come to you." And when those same disciples betray him and deny him and flee from his cross, his first act in resurrection is to give them forgiveness. "Peace," he pronounces to them, "peace be with you." Then he breathes upon them the Holy Spirit to give them his presence always with them. Our loves are "out of sight, out of mind," says Gerard Manley Hopkins. But Christ always minds; his interest eyes us, heart wants us, care haunts us, foot follows—kind. And he is "our ransom, our rescue, our first, fast, last friend."[22]

I don't know how you feel, but there is some glad, quiet joy about finding God in Jesus of Nazareth, because you see, we never have to be ashamed of him, and we never have to defend him. His own glory and grace shine through, like a light in the midst of the darkness, and even Pontius Pilate has to admit at the end: This man was the king. "I pray thee, Lord, show me thy glory," Moses asked of God. Well, we have seen his glory, full of grace and truth. The mists of mystery have been rolled back, good Christians; the really real has been revealed. God, Creator, Sustainer, Ultimate Power behind all this universe, is made known in the Son. Christ is the way, our New Testament lesson tells us; if we search for God, we find him in Jesus. He is the truth, the Revealer of that One who is ultimately real, beyond all other reality.

And he is not some amorphous spirit, some mystical om, some diffuse soul in nature—some great dumb thing that we dimly sense, but can never really know. He is not some consuming power to be feared and propitiated, but never ever loved. He is not some all-absorbing void into which we must dissolve, leaving our particular personality, our calling, our cares and labors in the world behind. Nor is he uncaring tyrant, to whom we play the puppets. And he certainly is not unconcerned benevolence, for whom anything goes.

No, we know better than all of that now. We have seen the Father in Jesus Christ, and we have heard all his commandments. We have seen him attending a wedding at Cana and talking with a divorced woman beside a well. We have seen him weeping with Mary and Martha beside the tomb of their brother Lazarus. We have watched him ride into Jerusalem on a donkey, and we have seen him on trial before the power of Rome. We have watched him die on a cross as soldiers gambled for his garments. And yes, we have met him alive in a garden, at the first rays of Easter morn, and we have traced with the finger of Thomas the marks of the nails in his risen hands. And because of that sacred story, we have confessed, "My Lord and my God!" By the way of Christ, through the truth of him, we have seen the Father.

Is it not glad announcement, then, that he wants to give us life—that there is not at the heart of this universe some mocking mask of evil, some demon of death who dangles us on the strings of our suffering—but rather that the mystery beyond all mysteries is a love who will not let us go, and who desires, no matter what it costs him, that we have life and have it more abundantly? That is the God revealed in the words and deeds of Jesus Christ—a God of life: common, everyday life on this earth, filled with mirth and the sound of laughter; life for you, ordered life, filled with the satisfactions of purposeful work and quiet rest; meaningful life and peaceable life, beyond the sordid victories of violence and wrong; loving life that reaches out in mercy to its neighbors; triumphant life that even death itself cannot destroy, but that abides and abides in the Father's house, though heaven and earth pass away. I am come that you might have life, Jesus told us, and then he spelled out for us the way of life in teaching after teaching. And he bid us follow him into that wholeness and goodness of the Father. He is the way to the Father, and the truth of him, and therefore the life, because he reveals the Person and the will of the Father, who is the source of all life.

When my husband and I were students at Basel University in Switzerland, we sat every week in the lectures of the great theologian, Karl Barth. He was a rumpled, lovable, old giant of learning, humble and joyful as such giants often are. One day as he read to us from the original manuscript of the *Church Dogmatics*, he paused in midsentence and grasped a strand of his disheveled white hair. "There is not a lock of the hair on my head," he exclaimed, "that is not infinitely interesting to God!" And that, good

Christians, is the mystery beyond all mysteries in this universe. There is nothing about you that is not infinitely interesting to God. And there is nothing other that he desires to do for you than to lead you into his life abundant.

The response to that is rather simple. Trust him. Trust the God revealed to you in Jesus Christ. Trust that the most real thing in this life of ours is not its suffering and its pain and its wrong, but the grace and mercy revealed to us in the glory of our crucified Lord. Trust that he knows the way to life in the Father, because he is the way. And then follow, follow daily what he has commanded you. Trust that his is the truth beyond all the distortions and degradations in our society. Trust that he is risen from the grave and can give you eternal life. Trust his love to give you abundant life here and now. Trust Jesus Christ. For he has truly shown us the Father, and yes, that is enough.

Amen.

D. Preaching for Epiphany (continued)

Topical and doctrinal sermons, in contrast to those that grow out of a single biblical book or passage, rest upon the witness of the entire canon of Scripture, because their purpose is to present the biblical perspective in relation to some topic of the day or to some doctrine. The doctrinal sermon that follows is, therefore, full of biblical quotations and allusions, ranging widely over both Old and New Testaments. In such a subject-sermon, any biblical material that illumines the discussion at hand may be used, although the preacher always has to be careful not to misinterpret passages of Scripture that have been lifted out of their context: obviously, in order to preach a topical or doctrinal sermon, the homiletician must be well versed in Bible.

This does not mean, however, that topical and doctrinal sermons are not also preached from specific texts. It is always distressing to find, in some book of sermons, a general treatment of a topic or of a theological subject for which no Scripture lesson is cited. The lack of a text means that the preacher has followed his or her own progression of thought in the sermon—worst of all, it usually means that the preacher is preaching his or her own opinions on the subject, and those, of course, carry no authority whatsoever. Either our preaching and our theology grow out of the biblical witness or they are so much vanity and empty wind. The following sermon carefully expounds both Old and New Testament texts, moving from the revelation of God at Sinai to the revelation of the same God in Jesus Christ, and focusing specifically on the testimonies in Scripture to his mystery, his power, and his demands. The Exodus passage and its context give most of the content to the first half of the sermon; the Hebrews passage and Hebrews' christological and ecclesiastical doctrines are the wellsprings of the second half. For example, Hebrews' emphases on Jesus' mediatorial function and its figures of the "cloud of witnesses" and of the pilgrim church are prominently used. This is theological preaching, because the Scriptures on which it is based are highly theological.

The sermon, which was first preached before seminary students and faculty in Watts Chapel at Union Theological Seminary in Richmond, grew out of the desire to expand the congregation's understanding of the act of worship. In our nonliturgical churches, the worship of Almighty God sometimes deteriorates into an hour concentrated solely on the human. The presence of the transcendent, holy God is forgotten. The participation of the worshipers in the coming kingdom of God and in the communion of saints is unknown. The focus of the whole becomes the preacher's words and his or her interaction with and persuasion of the listening congregation. Especially is this true when, as in some English Reformed traditions, there is so little symbolism in the sanctuary to remind the congregation of the presence of the triune God. In such a situation, it is the preacher's responsibility to remind them—to recall them to the true purpose and nature of worship. And strangely enough, in carrying out that responsibility, the preacher must die to self. That is, he or she must purposely turn aside a worship practice that has glorified the person in the pulpit, and prompt the congregation to glorify God instead.

In the New Testament text from the Epistle to the Hebrews that is used for this sermon, there is strong emphasis on the communion of saints, and therefore the section in this sermon that deals with that subject is treating a central doctrine of the Christian faith. That doctrine, however, is one that few of our parishioners understand. This sermon attempts to define that communion in very personal and vivid terms, as a fellowship in which the worshiping congregation is involved. But the sermon also then moves on to spell out the implications of the communion of saints for our daily lives—the assurance it gives, the demand it lays upon us, the guidance it affords.

The conclusion of the sermon does what conclusions ought to do—namely, sum up the thought of the entire sermon and call for the desired response from the congregation.

It should also be added that because this sermon was preached to a seminary congregation, there are allusions to figures and incidents in the Bible that would be totally incomprehensible to the average congregation. Most of our people would not have the foggiest notion of who Uzzah was, for example, or why he died when he touched the ark. Had I preached this sermon to a group of average lay persons, I would have used more familiar illustrations. But the sermon was also preached, in a somwhat altered form, at Massanetta Springs Bible Conference, and it was clearly received by lay persons educated in the Scriptures. Would that all our congregations so knew their Bible!

Sample Sermon:

OUR ORDINARY WORSHIP

Scripture: Exodus 19:10-19
Hebrews 12:18-29

Our worship in this place is a rather ordinary affair, and we have intentionally designed it that way. In the long history of the Christian Church, a lot of trappings and embellishments have accumulated around the practice of worship, but we have purposely eliminated most of them. When we come into this chapel, we do not cross ourselves or kneel in our pews, but rather seat ourselves comfortably. As we look around, we see no altar, no candles, no massive cross upon which to fix our gaze; we can instead observe our neighbors and see who has come to service. We have here no different light, filtered through brilliant stained-glass windows, and thus no sign that this place participates in another world. Watts Chapel remains very much the ordinary hall that it is. Those who lead the service here are not dressed in special vestments, but in the black gown or the street clothes proper to informality. Sometimes, when the preacher rises to begin the service, he even says "Good evening" or "Good morning" to us, in a folksy way. Yes, our worship in this ordinary hall is an ordinary, almost casual affair, and we have no intention of changing it or of trying to make it extraordinary.

Before we settle down and relax for a snooze in our pews, however, now that the hymns and prayers are over, let us consider the fact that we have come in here to worship God, and the God we worship is by no means any ordinary god. Israel found that out at Sinai. In the Old Testament lesson which we heard from the Scripture, that ragged bunch of Semitic slaves had made good their escape from Egypt, and then, bickering and griping, sometimes hungering and thirsting, occasionally fighting enemies, they had stumbled their way across the desert to the mountain where it had been promised to Moses that they would meet their Redeemer. God was descending to Mt. Sinai to confront all his people for the very first time—and believe me, if the God who descended to Sinai is the One who descends here into our midst tonight, then you and I are in for some surprises. It just may be that we should not be quite so comfortable and casual in this place. It just may be that this seemingly ordinary room is the abode of a living and consuming fire, and that you and I are in danger of our lives. As Amos Wilder put it in a poem:

Going to church is like approaching an open volcano
where the world is molten
and hearts are sifted.
The altar is like a third rail that spatters sparks,
the sanctuary is like the chamber next the atomic oven:
there are invisible rays and you leave your watch outside.[23]

God descends to be here in our midst tonight—"The Lord is
in his holy temple." God descends, as he descended to
Sinai, and nothing here is ordinary.

There is mystery here, if the God of Sinai is present—the
mystery of his presence, which we simply cannot describe,
the mystery of a reality unlike anything in all creation. The
Old Testament writers try to describe God; incredibly, some
of them say they actually saw him. "I saw the Lord," Isaiah
writes, "sitting upon a throne, high and lifted up." Or later
in our exodus story, we are told that the elders of Israel
ascended Sinai, and beheld God, and ate and drank with
him, in the Old Testament equivalent of the Lord's Supper.
But the same writers cannot describe the mystery of the
being of God. They can only tell us about the fantastic things
that accompanied him—the seraphim and the kingly robe
and the burning coal in Isaiah—the clear pavement of
sapphire stone in the ancient supper on Sinai. So too is it
with that descent of God to Sinai: we hear only of what
accompanies his presence as he descends to earth to be with
his people—thunders and lightnings and a thick cloud and
a deafening trumpet blast—the strange and bizarre symbols
of his holy presence.

We would like to turn it all into a natural and ordinary
event, of course, in order that we may deal with it. It was
just a volcanic eruption at Sinai, say some commentators,
from an ordinary mountain. But God's entrance into this
world is never ordinary, and if you demythologize Sinai
then you've still got to deal with Ezekiel's wheels in wheels,
and that awful antiphonal song that Isaiah heard: "Holy,
holy, holy," as the thresholds of the temple quaked and the
sanctuary filled with smoke. Or you have to think about
Amos' God, with the mountains melting before him, or the

smoking firepot and flaming torch in the covenant with Father Abraham.

That's the God who has invaded our worship here tonight, and turned this ordinary room into a holy place. And you and I are here before the mystery of his presence.

We are here before his power, too, if the God of Sinai has descended to this room—power so great that it set the mountains to skipping like rams, to use the psalmist's language, after the Reed Sea had looked and fled and Jordan had turned back. Do you think you can remain alive in the presence of such power? Uzzah touched just the holy ark, the base of the throne of God, and died on the spot. Israel is warned—wash your garments, do not touch the border of the mountain, be ready by the third day. There descends here into the midst of our worship the God of holy power, whose breath withers or makes alive, whose word ignited the sun, who shakes the earth and sifts the nations, and measures the seas in the palm of his hand.

Were we ready to confront such power when we came in here tonight, and can we relax in our pews in the presence of it? Or do we need rather some trembling concern for what it may do with us? Israel trembled and was afraid and begged Moses to speak to God for her. Have we come in here lightly and glibly to pray to such holy power? "The Lord reigns; let the peoples tremble," the psalmist admonishes us. You and I are here before the God of holy power.

And yes, we are here before God's demand, too, if the God of Sinai is present in this place, because the God of Israel did not descend to the mountain just to give his people a worship experience. He descended to speak to them a word, and the word laid his ultimate claim upon their lives: "You shall have no other gods before me." That was a word which changed Israel's entire existence. She no longer had the freedom, you see, to chart her own course or to lay her own plans for the future. She no longer could do as they did in Egypt or in Canaan, to which she was going. Now she had to renounce her world and do as God commanded. "You shall not bow down and serve anything that is in the heaven above or the earth beneath, or that is in the water under the earth." Israel no longer could find her God in the processes or the wonders of nature or in the movements of the stars. Now she had to know him solely in his acts and in the words he spoke to her. Indeed, Israel could not even know herself as a natural people, bound together by ties of blood or soil or economic interest. "You shall be to me a kingdom of priests and a holy nation." Now Israel had only one unity—the unity of her shared redemption out of slavery in Egypt—and if she forgot her exodus and the God who caused it, she ceased to be a people. "Hear, O Israel: The Lord our God is one Lord; and you shall love the Lord your God with all your heart, and with all your soul, and with all your might." That was the demand which the God of Sinai laid upon his people. And it is the demand laid upon us, too, here tonight, if the God of Israel is present with us.

No, our worship here tonight is not an ordinary affair, because the God who is present in our midst is not an ordinary God. And so, says Wilder, at the end of his poem, we come in here, not to be tranquilized but exorcised:

> Follow the pillar of fire and the pillar of cloud
> with exultation and abandon,
> with fear and trembling,
> for the zeal of the Lord of Hosts . . .
> waits not on the circumspect
> and the flames of love
> both bless and consume.[24]

The God of Sinai is present here, and that God is a mysterious, powerful, demanding, consuming fire.

Is that too much to bear, friends? Do you find it impossible to deal with a God whose being you cannot fathom, whose mysterious presence makes the hair on the back of your neck stand up and your throat feel dry? Do you feel puny and insignificant before the power which whirls the galaxies around and yet demands that you love him? And do you know that you can never satisfy the demands of such a God, or worship him truly? Do you wish, in short, that you could hide from such a God and forget all about

Sinai, and just keep Watts Chapel the same ordinary and friendly place that you once thought it was? Well, so do I, because I do not know how I can stand before such a God, much less sit before him. I find myself looking frantically about for some place to kneel every time I come in here and think of Sinai. And even then, I know I don't have a prayer to my name. "Who can endure the day of his coming? asks Malachi about this God who is like a refiner's fire. I can't endure it; I'm sure of that. No one of us can.

Perhaps then we need very much the word of our New Testament lesson. For it tells us that between us and the time of God's descent to Sinai, God came also in his Son, and that now there stands between us and our Creator the figure of a cross. "You have not come to what may be touched," it reads, "a blazing fire, and darkness, and gloom, and a tempest, and the sound of a trumpet, and a voice whose words made the hearers entreat that no further messages be spoken to them . . . Indeed, so terrifying was the sight that Moses said, 'I tremble with fear!' But you have come . . . to Jesus, the mediator of a new covenant, and to the sprinkled blood that speaks more graciously than the blood of Abel." We have come here in our worship first of all to Jesus. It is he who is in our midst, and because he has died and risen again and mediates for us as we pray and praise in this place, the God of Sinai hears our prayers and accepts our praise and allows us to appear before him and still live. For Jesus' sake, who is with us tonight, God accepts our worship. The Epistle to the Hebrews never tires of telling us that: we may, with confidence, draw near to the throne of grace, and receive mercy and find grace to help in time of need, it says. We may, with confidence, enter the sanctuary by the blood of Jesus, and draw near to God in full assurance of faith.

We have come to Jesus! What a relief that is!—to get rid of all that fire and thundering, and to deal with the friendly things of earth again—to get out of the realm of mystery and power and impossible demand and to deal with the man from Nazareth. "Gentle Jesus, meek and mild!"—a person can relax around him. "Amazing grace! How sweet the sound!"—it lets us return to being just human beings, and Watts Chapel can return to being the ordinary place that it is.

Is that the temptation we have, once we have heard the word of the gospel—to think that now we are done with Sinai and have only to do with the commonplace? If it is, then we had better listen again to what our New Testament lesson has to say to us, for it is precisely the God of Sinai whose word is spoken to us in his Son Jesus Christ, and in Christ we are confronted even more fully by that which we cannot comprehend, by one who has all power in heaven and on earth, by one who lays his command upon us.

To be sure, we now know what God is like. The veil of the temple in truth has been rent in two and we have passed into the holy of holies. We have seen the light of the knowledge of the glory of God shining in the face of Christ. We now know who the Father is: he is pure and undimmed love, shining in our darkness, illumining our hearts, burning clean our soiled and rusted spirits. But that he should love the likes of you and me, that he should guard our every moment, that he should number the hairs on our heads, and listen here to our mumbled and selfish prayers—that, that is a mystery which I cannot comprehend. Or more, that that Father should give up his own Son and let us nail him to a tree, just because he wants all people to have joy forever—

> See, from his head, his hands, his feet,
> Sorrow and love flow mingled down!
> Did e'er such love and sorrow meet,
> Or thorns compose so rich a crown?[25]

Oh no, that is a deed I simply cannot understand, and though we gaze into the heart of God by means of the cross of Jesus Christ, the love revealed there becomes for us more of a mystery than Sinai ever was. And that, that One, you see, is the Lord we worship here tonight in this ordinary place.

And his power! Just think of his power! The blind receive their sight and the lame walk, lepers are cleansed and the deaf hear, and the dead are raised up by his holy presence. But more than that, he has wrestled with the forces of chaos and death and hell itself and now stands in our midst—alive!

Then even more than that, did you catch in our New Testament reading the completed outcome of his power? Listen again to what Hebrews tells us about our worship in this place: "You have come to Mt. Zion," it says, "and to the city of the living God, the heavenly Jerusalem, and to innumerable angels in festal gathering, and to the assembly of the first-born who are enrolled in heaven, and to a judge who is God of all, and to the spirits of just men made perfect, and to Jesus." In other words, we sit here in Watts Chapel in the company of the communion of saints in the eternal kingdom. Christ has triumphed, the battle has been won, the victory is now assured. By his life and death and resurrection, Jesus Christ has begun the kingdom of God; and by our faith in him, and our worship of him, we participate here in its perfection. Think of it! All those faithful souls of the past who went out, not knowing where they were going—all those who by faith sojourned in the land of promise—all those who looked forward to the city which has foundations, whose builder and maker is God—all that splendid host of the past is here at the end of the journey. Shall we say that they look down at us, that cloud of witnesses, from the balcony? Abraham over there to the right, Isaiah in the middle, and Amos on the left above, staring at the back of your neck? Is Calvin there in the second row, and Luther on the other side? And is that not Augustine and Thomas Aquinas, and St. Francis beside them? We come here in our worship to Jesus, and through him, to God's powerful purpose completed. We participate here in this supposedly ordinary room in nothing less than the kingdom of God.

Do you know what that means for the life we lead in our daily round? It means that all the work and caring and learning and struggling that we're doing in our communities and in our churches will not be in vain. The kingdom comes. It has already begun. Our work and trust, if they are faithful, will bear their fruit. And here in our worship, in this common place, because of Jesus, we taste the first fruits already.

Need I tell you, then, that here with Jesus we still stand under a divine command? As Hebrews puts it earlier in the chapter, this is no time for "drooping hands" and "weak knees." This is the time to run the race that is set before us. We now know, you and I, just where our world is going to end up. We know the kingdom of God is coming, because here in our worship, we stand already with one foot in heaven. Is not our task, then, to tell the rest of the world about what has been made known to us? "Go ye into all the world and preach the gospel!"—the divine command is laid upon us. And Hebrews adds, "See that you do not refuse him who is speaking."

If we want to know just what to do and how to go about our mission, if we need some instruction in how to live as the people of God, then we have here in our worship that whole company of saints in whose fellowship we abide. And our time in the classrooms of this seminary and in our church schools should be devoted to studying their witness and actions, because from them we can learn very clearly what it means to be faithful.

Above all, there stands in our midst our crucified and risen Savior. The marks of the nails are still there in his hands, and the cut of the spear in his side. His brow still shows the scratches from the thorns and his lips are still dry from the thirst. He looks at each one of us, with burning eyes of compassion, and he speaks his demand: "A new commandment I give unto you, that you love one another; even as I have loved you".

Yes, we are confronted here in this sacred place still, as Israel was confronted on Sinai, with God's mystery and God's power and God's absolute demand. They come to us through Jesus Christ, who was dead and yet who now is alive and who stands here among us. Let us therefore offer to him acceptable worship, with reverence and awe. And then let us go out and tell the world what we have known in this holy room. Amen.

E. Preaching for Lent

Lent is the season in the church year that emphasizes repentance, discipline, and preparation for baptism into the death of Christ, that we may be raised to newness of life. Lent originated in the church year as that time when new converts to the Christian faith were instructed in the catechism and underwent special disciplines of fasting, prayer, and Bible study to prepare them for their entrance on Easter into the Body of Christ through baptism. But Lenten practices quickly spread to all the faithful as efficacious ways of renewing their commitment to the new life in Christ Jesus.

I therefore have placed the following sermon under the rubric of Lent, because it emphasizes the exercises of will and heart and mind that are necessary for the Christian to appropriate the redemption given us in our Lord. The sermon also would be appropriate to the season of Pentecost, of course, and that was actually when it was first preached—before a summer congregation gathered for Monday morning worship in the huge amphitheater of Chautauqua Institution, New York. Since that time, however, I have frequently used it as a Lenten message.

This sermon wrestles with one of the most difficult theological problems of the Christian faith: the relation of our works, as men and women *already redeemed* by the cross and resurrection, to the appropriation of our final salvation. There is no doubt, in the Christian faith, that we are freed from our slavery to sin and death solely by the work of God in Jesus Christ. But then many questions arise: Do we still have something to do? By our manner of life, in response to God's act in Christ, do we either accept or reject God's saving grace? And if we can reject his grace, does that mean that our redemption is annulled and that we are forever lost? Basically, the questions all have to do with the doctrine of election and with the problem of whether or not God's election can be annulled by our continuing unfaithfulness and disobedience and failure to appropriate its benefits.

In some branches of the Reformed faith, there is no doubt

about the answer to these questions. *The Westminster Confession* is sure, for example, that God's election cannot be annulled by our unfaithfulness and that his grace will triumph in the end and give eternal life:

They whom God hath accepted in his Beloved, effectually called and sanctified by his Spirit, can neither totally nor finally fall away from the state of grace; but shall certainly persevere therein to the end, and be eternally saved. (XIX.1)

Nevertheless they may, through the temptations of Satan and of the world, the prevalency of corruption remaining in them, and the neglect of the means of their preservation, fall into grievous sins; and for a time continue therein: whereby they incur God's displeasure, and grieve his Holy Spirit; come to be deprived of some measure of their graces and comforts; have their hearts hardened, and their consciences wounded; hurt and scandalize others, and bring temporal judgments upon themselves. (XIX.3) God doth continue to forgive the sins of those that are justified: and, although they can never fall from the state of justification, yet they may by their sins fall under God's Fatherly displeasure, and not have the light of his countenance restored unto them until they humble themselves, confess their sins, beg pardon, and renew their faith and repentance. (XIII.5)

Thus, life on this earth, even of the elect, can be a living hell, because it is life lived under God's displeasure. Nevertheless, God's election is irrevocable and the elect will enter the kingdom.

On the other side, the confessions of the church must be measured by the teaching of the Scriptures, and there is much in the New Testament that would lead us to believe that the benefits of our redemption in Christ can be lost to us. To give only a few examples, we find Paul writing to the Corinthian Christians, "Do you not know that you are God's temple and that God's Spirit dwells in you? If anyone destroys God's temple, God will destroy him" (I Corinthians 3:16-17). Those who have been given the Spirit at baptism and thus have been justified and redeemed can yet be condemned. In Galatians 5:4, Paul specifically states that those who have received Christ and who then turn aside to follow the law can fall away from grace. But most amazingly, the apostle writes of himself, "I pommel my body and subdue it, lest after preaching to others I myself should be disqualified" (1 Corinthians 9:27). This towering apostle knows that it is possible even for him to lose the prize of eternal life (cf. Philippians 3:12-16). Similarly, the writer of Hebrews warns Christians not to follow the practice of Israel by hardening their hearts "as in the wilderness": "For we share in Christ, if only we hold our first confidence firm to the end" (3:14) . . . "Therefore, while the promise of entering his rest remains, let us fear lest any of you be judged to have failed to reach it" (4:1).

The Scriptures critique and correct the theology of the church, and in the development of any sermon, the preacher must pay attention to both. In one sense, *The Westminster Confession* is not wrong: by its doctrine of election, it is affirming the faithfulness of God to his electing Word, his ability to overcome all human sin by his active grace, and the positive assurance and comfort that that faithfulness and power give to the sincere Christian. The Scriptures, on the other hand, prevent the indifferent Christian from taking God's electing grace for granted, from entering into a life of slothful disobedience, and from thereby mocking God's love.

These latter concerns are the subject of the following sermon. It is directed at those Christians who rely on "cheap grace," to use Bonhoeffer's phrase—who think to enjoy the benefits of redemption by God through Jesus Christ without responding to them—and of course the number of such Christians is legion. Often we ourselves are numbered among them. Our indifference becomes manifest when we start thinking that eternal life is automatically given at death—as do so many in our society—or when we assure ourselves that God accepts us even when we ignore his gospel, or when we assume that we can love God and at the same time hate our brother or spouse or acquaintance. When we rely on such cheap grace, we become like Israel, who enjoyed her release from slavery and her entrance into a new life of freedom without responding to that mercy in faith and obedience.

Indeed, it is that parallel of our Christian life with Israel's life after her release from captivity in Egypt, that determines the form and content of this sermon. The congregation, as the new Israel in Christ, is enabled to identify with Israel in the Old Testament, and to see Israel's journey and choice as its own. Such a hermeneutic is consistent with both Old and New Testaments: Deuteronomy views succeeding generations of Israelites as participants in the earlier redemption out of Egypt (cf. Deuteronomy 29:10-15); portions of the New Testament see the church as the new Israel of God (Galatians 6:16), whose pilgrimage parallels that of the old Israel.

However, this sermon not only proclaims the message of its texts—that there is a response which must be made to the mercy of God—but it also emphasizes, in its concluding section, that unfailing faithfulness and love of God, with which *The Westminster Confession's* doctrine of election is concerned. The call to love God is set, in the sermon, in the context of God's love and of his constant, never-failing guidance and sustenance of us. The sermon, therefore, tries to reach that balance between God's grace and our response to it, which is finally characteristic of the Scriptures, and which is perhaps best summed up in Paul's direction to his beloved church at Philippi: "Therefore, my beloved, as you have always obeyed, so now, not only as in my presence but much more in my absence, work out your own salvation with fear and trembling; for God is at work in you, both to will and to work for his good pleasure" (2:12-13). We must work, but it is God who is at work within us.

I have set forth this rather lengthy theological preface to this sermon to show the dialogue with church theology and Scripture that should constantly take place in the preacher's mind as a sermon is developed. The preacher should always be aware of how his or her sermon relates to theology and Bible, and of how the teachings of both are being set forth in the Sunday message. Only if such awareness is present, can the homiletician be assured that the sermon is in fact Christian.

Sample Sermon:

THE JOURNEY—THE CHOICE

Scripture: Deuteronomy 30:15-20
Matthew 7:13-29

"I call heaven and earth to witness against you this day, that I have set before you life and death, blessing and curse; therefore choose life, that you and your descendants may live. . . ."

Deuteronomy 30:19

You and I are now on a journey through life, traveling somewhere between a time when we were enslaved and captive, and a time when we shall enter into our final fulfillment and salvation.

So it was with Israel, to whom Moses spoke the words in our text. She had been a captive people in Egypt, enslaved to the Pharaoh, and forced to toil at making bricks for his royal building projects. But that all lay behind Israel now. She had been rescued out of slavery. She had wandered for forty years through the dry and desolate desert. But now finally at last she stood on the eastern side of the Jordan, looking across to the promised land, which flowed with milk and honey. Now she had arrived at a point in time between captivity and a future abundant life. Now she moved in her pilgrimage away from enslavement toward her salvation.

That is the description of our lives, too, is it not? We may think our days are aimless wandering from one thing to the next—beset simply with our little problems and struggles to find our own happiness. We may think that there is nothing behind us but our own particular biographies—childhood, youth, education, jobs—interspersed here and there with a war or some other slice from history. We may think there is nothing ahead but the completion of some task we have set for ourselves—bringing up the kids, earning a promotion, turning out the product, keeping the household running smoothly.

106

I once asked an acquaintance, an engineering executive for a pharmaceutical company, "George, what's the purpose of your life?" to which he replied in so many words, "It has no purpose, except to design machines that will turn out Band-Aids faster." Thus trivial and aimless and meaningless our lives can seem at time—as if they were measured out in coffee spoons at home, or in production figures at the office.

But the truth is that now you and I have moved out on a fateful journey, traveling a road on which the Lord God has set us in his purpose. And we got started on the journey, on this soul-size pilgrimage, by being rescued out of slavery.

We were once enslaved to the power of death, were we not? What one of us here can deny that? Death has hung over the human race like some great phantom from the beginning of our first disobedience. The final last insult to all the aspirations of the human personality, the great leveller of all our claims to pomp and glory, the inevitable end of every good dream and every loving relationship— death has held human beings captive, in fear, to its tyrannical void and oblivion. And try as we will to escape its clutches, we never can outrun its grasp or loose its cold fingers from encircling our lives and the lives of all whom we love. We cannot. But God did, in the resurrection of Jesus Christ. At the site of that empty tomb on Easter morn, death's tyranny was broken. There human flesh and blood were delivered from the grave's captivity, and the awful phantom of death forever lost the power to claim humanity as its slave. "O death, where is thy sting? O grave, where is thy victory?" God has now delivered you and me and all humanity from enslavement to the power of death.

So, too, he has delivered us all from slavery to the power of evil. I think so often of an alcoholic friend of mine, who keeps drinking because he has to forget. His marriage is a shambles, his self-respect gone, he only goes through the motions on his job. But he has done so many terrible things to his loved ones while drunk that he can no longer stand being sober. And so, slave to his guilt and his own sin, he goes around a vicious treadmill, drinking even more in the vain attempt to drown out memory.

Most of us are not alcoholics, but are we not all captive to some dark memory of which we would like to be free?—the memory of a marriage ruined, a friend wounded, a child misguided? The memory of foolishness, of pride, of narrow self-seeking? Indeed, the memory of the whole human race is so stained with blood and violence and suffering inflicted on the defenseless, that we seem ever destined to be slaves to the consequences of humanity's collective evil.

But a new power invaded history's scene in the cross of Jesus Christ, and since that sacrifice we have all had a chance at a totally new beginning. With Christ's blood, flowing for us all, the evil of the past was washed away, and the purifying spirit of a new creation came flooding into human life. God in his Son cleansed the stains of polluting evil, and humanity now has been given the possibility of deliverance from slavery to its own guilty past.

You and I and all people have been redeemed out of captivity. And now we are traveling on God's road, which leads toward some final fulfillment. We are all Israel, good Christians, standing now east of the Jordan—our Egypts behind us, and the possibility of an abundant life out there ahead. God has come meddling in our private lives, through Jesus Christ, changing their circumstances. He rescued us. He redeemed us. He bought us back. In Christ our Lord, he claimed us as his own. And so the road we travel is now his road, leading from redemption toward the future.

But what that future is depends largely now on some decisions we have to make. Like Israel, we have the possibility of a new abundant life. The power has been given in Christ our Lord to lead a free, full existence. But now we have to respond to that power, and appropriate it and make it our own. Now we have to practice living as redeemed men and women.

We Christians sometimes kid ourselves into thinking that because Christ has died and risen from the dead, we have nothing else to do. We glibly imagine that from now on we shall just float down the stream of grace, and somehow automatically drift into the benefits of our salvation. But our Scripture lessons for the morning tell us otherwise. We walk a road, they remind us, and in Jesus' words, "The gate is narrow and the way is hard, that leads to life, and those who find it are few." Having been rescued out of slavery by his blessed sacrifice, you and I can fail to find any blessing. Having been redeemed by the cross and empty tomb, we can still fail to realize the full benefits of our redemption.

That would be a terrible mistake to make, because God in his love has planned such an abundant future for us.

We have lots of supposed saviors on the scene these days—our New Testament lesson would call them false prophets, ravenous wolves in sheep's clothing. And they all promise us some sort of fulfillment for our lives. We can get our heads together, they tell us, or we can become total women. We can learn how to win through intimidation, or we can become o.k. We can get "it" through EST and realize that we are perfect just the way we are. Or we can unleash the "true selves" within us and find that we are divine. Did you read the interview with pop singer John Denver in *Newsweek* some time ago? "I reflect in a very real way where humanity is—where we're going," Denver said. And he's sampled all the savior cults—TM, yoga, Rolfing, EST, pyramid power, and astrology. "I can do anything," said Denver. "One of these days I'll be so complete I won't be a human. I'll be a god."[26]

How hollow and ludicrous that sounds when you put it up against the life promised to us in Jesus Christ! "The fruit of the Spirit," writes Paul, "is love, joy, peace, patience, kindness, goodness, faithfulness, gentleness, self-control." The abundant life God holds out before us has all those qualities. Can you picture the transformation they could work in our society, or in your home or mine? That we could learn to be patient with one another, and kind, and gentle, and self-controlled? That we, midst all the troubles of life, could find some inner joy, and a peace passing understanding that the world neither gives nor can ever take away? Truly, the abundant life God wants for us is life as it was meant to be lived.

But you and I, this day, now choose that life, or fall victim again to death and evil. "I call heaven and earth to witness against you this day," says our Scripture, "that I have set before you life and death, blessing and curse; therefore choose life, that you and your descendants may live. . . ."

So we need to examine this morning how to go about choosing life, how so to conduct ourselves that we may enter into that good future that lies out there before us.

Our Old Testament text first of all gives us help in telling us what to do. We can choose life, it says, by loving the Lord our God, by obeying his voice, and by cleaving to him. But that really is not much different from what we heard also from Jesus: "Not every one who says to me, 'Lord, Lord', shall enter the kingdom of heaven, but he who does the will of my Father who is in heaven." And then there is that comparison: "Every one then who hears these words of mine and does them will be like a wise man who built his house upon the rock."

In other words, the Scriptures are quite convinced that we can have life only by falling in love with God. But they are equally sure that we love God only by being obedient to him. And really, how else should it be when we are talking about love? Love is not primarily an emotion; love is an action—as any happily married man or woman knows to the depths of his or her being. Love is not primarily a feeling; love is a living relationship. It is the most strenuous willing and effort to bring two lives into harmony as one, the day-by-day striving to communicate and share and care, the deliberate effort to walk along the same path together, the conscious labor to maintain the most intimate communion. And that, say our Scripture lessons, is the love we are to have for God.

We live in an age and a society where anything goes. If It Feels Good, Do It, read the bumper stickers. And so anarchy has invaded our personal lives, with everyone doing his or her thing. It is like that sad comment at the end of the Old Testament Book of Judges: "In those days there was no king in Israel; every man did what was right in his own eyes." There is no divine king anymore over our thoughts and actions; we all do what is right in our own eyes. But Israel lost her good life in the land of promise because that was the condition of her society. And we should be warned by the concrete, historical fate that followed her refusal to obey her God.

We choose life by loving the Lord, which means, by obeying him. We choose life by bringing our lives into harmony with his, by maintaining the most intimate relationship with him. We choose life, or we inherit death and curse. That is the plain, hard, realistic message of both Old and New Testament.

Then perhaps what we need to do is to begin to love and obey by trying to forgive others as God has forgiven us. He wiped out our past and gave us a new beginning with the sacrifice of his Son on the cross. To love him now therefore means to wipe out the evil past in our relations with those around us—the past resentment you have against your spouse that has been festering in your marriage for months, the past feud you have with a relative whom you have deliberately avoided, the past dispute you had with a friend that has broken the communion between you.

At our summer place in Pennyslvania, we live next door to a couple whose family has been split by a petty argument for four years. They got into a dispute with their brother and sister-in-law over who should clean the summer place. And now the relatives avoid one another and have never even seen each other's latest children. And that, good Christians, is the way of death and not the way of life. To love God means to forgive others as he has forgiven us.

Surely, too, to love our God means to care for those for whom he cares. Which means, I am sure, that even one wretched, disagreeable, or disreputable member of the human race cannot be shut out of the circle of our concern. There are a lot of people in this world who offend our sensibilities. There are those whose lives are totally repugnant to us. And yes, there is that vast body of the poor, the illiterate, the hungry, the diseased, whose problems never seem to be ended. At times we would just like to close our eyes and shut our ears to their need. But God cared so much for them that he sent his Son into their poverty and suffering:

> As one from whom men hide their faces
> he was despised, and we esteemed him not.

If we love God, we will care for all the despised and needy for whom he so much cares. His love will be our love, and his compassion our compassion.

Perhaps most important in the 1980s, if we love God, we will love one another with the faithfulness he has shown toward us. Our society is slowly being undermined these days by those who will not keep their covenants—those government officials who cynically violate the public trust, those businessmen and laborers who do not make reliable goods or give honest return for the consumer's money, those husbands or wives who consider their marriage a bond to be easily broken, those parents who turn over the responsibility for guiding their children to the TV set for hours on end, day after day. But if we would enter into abundant life in our generation, we will do so only by a renewal of our sense of responsibility, by faithfulness to the promises we make and the tasks we have said we will do—a faithfulness as unswerving and self-sacrificing as God's faithfulness to us in Jesus Christ.

We should have no illusions about what all that will cost us. "The way is hard, that leads to life," Jesus said. And in a society such as ours, where success is measured by how much money we have, and the media is telling us on every side that faithfulness is strictly for squares, and every huckster is urging us to look only to our own rights and happiness, it is not easy to love God by being forgiving and compassionate and faithful. It takes the most single-minded concentration on his will, as has been told to us by Jesus Christ. It takes the most vigorous exercise of self-discipline and of firm decision. It takes the most consistent turning to God in prayer and worship and study of the Scriptures, to find the power to keep us going. That is what Deuteronomy means when it tells us to cleave to the Lord. We cling to him! We are to cling to him for the power he gives, which will sustain us in obedience. Then slowly, surely, our lives will be shaped, and we will find ourselves in love with God.

It is hard to enter into life. But really, it is easy too. Because who can help loving the God who has brought us thus far on our journey. He has been by our side every step along the way. When we were still in our mother's womb, his hands shaped and fashioned us. In the marvelous words of Job, he clothed us with skin and flesh, and knit us together with bones and sinews. Day-by-day, he has sustained our breath and lavished on us his care—placing us in home and family, surrounding us with a world of wonder. Every morning his mercies are new, every evening his watch over us unfailing. When we walk through some dark valley of the shadow, underneath are his everlasting arms. When we know only joy and bright gaiety, he increases gladness by pouring out the glories of the morning, creating color and birdsong and light to aid us in celebration.

And now here we are, you and I, with that crucial decision before us. Will we love and obey and cleave to such a God, and thus enter into abundant life? Or will we choose the path that leads away from him and thus inevitably toward death and evil? We have come a long way on our soul-size journey—all the way from Egypt—bought out of slavery by the sacrifice of God's beloved Son. Such was the depth of God's love for us then. Such is the depth of the love he still offers. He holds out to us life and good and kindness and joy, in that fulfillment out there before us.

"See," God says, "I set before you this day life and good, death and evil." And one can almost hear the great voice, resonant with love, pleading from the great heart of mercy, "O my people, choose life this day! O my people, choose life!"

Amen.

F. Preaching for Eastertide

In some of our churches, our observances of Lent and Eastertide are seriously out of balance. Most of the churches in this country have some sort of Lenten observances that they carry on for the six weeks preceding Good Friday. Some of those churches then celebrate Holy Week, and above all, the crucifixion as the climax of that period. But Good Friday is by no means the climax of the church year. Easter is. The resurrection is the foundation of the Christian faith. Yet, many preachers devote only one Sunday to the celebration of Easter and then move on to other topics on the Sundays that follow.

To correct this imbalance, the liturgical year includes the season of Eastertide—seven Sundays on which the meaning of the resurrection for the life of God's people is to be especially explored.

The sermon that follows is just such an Eastertide sermon. It was first preached from the pulpit of Second Presbyterian Church, Richmond, Virginia, before an affluent, educated congregation. It is a doctrinal sermon, intended to explore the Christian view of death. As a doctrinal sermon, it draws on the canon as a whole, and yet its title and main theme are drawn from the lesson in 1 Corinthians, especially verse 26, and its final section centers about the meaning of the question in Luke 24:5, with much of the rest of its thought drawn from the context of those two Scripture verses.

When dealing with a central doctrine of the Christian faith that also is a part of universal human experience, such as death, the preacher should certainly acknowledge and deal with views found in society at large. This sermon treats current American approaches to death and to life-after-death at some length. They are not handled abstractly, but in personal terms where possible, in order that the congregation's own thoughts and feelings about death may come to the surface and be examined.

Then, significantly, the glad news of the resurrection also is proclaimed in the most personal terms, in order that its gospel may penetrate hearts and minds and feelings, and work its healing in them. The resurrection faith is not an abstract truth given to the church, and it must not be preached abstractly. First, it is based upon the church's two

114

thousand years of experience of the risen Lord in its midst. At the heart of all Christian doctrine, worship, and practice is a living fellowship with God, who is present in the midst of his people in Christ's Spirit. The church, therefore, has always spelled out its understandings in terms of that fellowship: sin is separation from God; reconciliation and atonement are return to him; Christ gives the new covenant by which we are forgiven and accepted once more into God's presence; Christ's mediation furnishes the means by which we may draw near in confidence to the throne of grace; the worship of the church presupposes that "where two or three are gathered together" in his name, there is Christ in the midst of them; and Christian living looks for its motivation and empowerment to the working of God's Spirit within individual Christian and church body. All, all depend on God's personal presence with his people in Christ's Spirit. The resurrection therefore proclaims that "neither death, nor life . . . nor anything else in all creation" (Romans 8:39) can now separate us from the presence of the triune God.

Second, this sermon proclaims the glad news of the resurrection in personal terms by spelling out the significance of that victory for each and every member of the congregation. Too often we preachers proclaim the resurrection of Jesus Christ without explaining what it means, and while our people may believe what we say, they may still be at an almost total loss to understand why it is so important. In three points, in its final section, this sermon tries to say why the resurrection is important. The language is made as arresting and as intimate as possible to drive home the meaning of Christ's victory. Yet, even then, this sermon's exposition of that meaning only scratches the surface of the significance of the resurrection. Much more could have been said, for example, about the victory of God in Christ over the world's evil. The triumph of God on Easter morn can be endlessly explored during the Sundays of Eastertide, because its meaning is inexhaustible and its effects are never at an end.

The sermon ends with my own very personal witness:

faith prompting faith. Preachers should not inject themselves too often into their sermons, lest they start glorifying
themselves and not God, and lest they begin preaching
their own thoughts and not the gospel. But there are times
when the preacher's personal testimony can be used to give
words to the congregation's thoughts and feelings. The
affirmation at the end of this sermon seemed to be one of
those times.

Sample Sermon:

DEALING WITH THE FINAL FOE

*Scripture: Luke 24:1-11
1 Corinthians 15:17-28*

Two Sundays ago, you heard from this pulpit the
proclamation of the Easter good news, the announcement
that Jesus Christ has been raised from the dead. And
certainly that is the central fact of the Christian faith, the
foundation on which the church stands, and without which
it falls. As Paul puts it, "If Christ has not been raised, your
faith is futile and you are still in your sins." Easter is not just
an appendix tacked on to the teachings of Jesus by which we
live, or on to the cross of Jesus by which we are forgiven.
No, Easter is the confirmation that the whole gospel is true,
and that therefore this life we have been given really is
worth living. As a result, the entire history of the church has
been an effort to understand fully the meaning of Easter,
and into the cycle of its sacred year, the church has built the
season of Eastertide, the time when we are especially to
explore the meaning of this event which has taken place.
Just as there are six Sundays in Lent leading up to the cross,
so there are seven Sundays in Eastertide leading away from
the empty tomb, and we are now at the third Sunday in that
holy season.

But isn't it significant that when we come in this season to
the very center of the Christian faith, we find ourselves
dealing with the issues of life and death? You and I are

rather superficial people at times. We worried about how
our new clothes looked when we got dressed for church this
morning. We are unhappy that we bought that latest block
of stock at 24¼, when if we had been on our toes, we could
have gotten it at 23. We nag at the kids at school, because the
course they are following is not sufficiently feeding our
parental pride. But here, now, in this Eastertide we are
concerned with life and death—with whether those
youngsters of ours are even going to continue to have a
world to live in after we are gone, or whether this planet is
going to be nothing but a burned out ash, floating dead and
silent through space. We are concerned here in Eastertide
with those cemeteries on the edge of town, and with
whether or not there is anything beyond their gates and
graves: Have you noticed how so many of them mark their
entrance roads with the sign, No Exit? We are concerned
here at Eastertime with whether there is any lasting
meaning and purpose to it all, or whether finally, as
Jeremiah puts it, "death has come up into our windows,"
and now sits in our living rooms, waiting to cut off every
love we hold for one another; every project so carefully
planned and started; every good work achieved by our
labor; every hopeful and lovely dream for the future. The
Christian faith has brought us down to the nitty-gritty of
living now, and we are dealing with the basic issue: death or
life, grief or good, futility or meaning.

It is exactly as Paul says it is. "The last enemy to be
destroyed is death." Here at the heart of the Christian faith,
we face the final foe.

Of course death doesn't always appear to us as an enemy.
For those who have lived a full life to a ripe old age, who die
surrounded by loved ones and honor, and with the
satisfaction of a life well-lived, death comes as an almost
natural part of life, the expected switching off of biological
cells, one by one. As the Bible writes of Abraham,
"Abraham breathed his last and died in a good old age, an
old man and full of years, and was gathered to his people."
There is something very gentle and natural about that.

Then again, death can be a release for some—a release

from pain or poverty or tragedy. Even those who commit suicide hope for something better. Dr. Kübler-Ross tells us that the poor often die rather peacefully. It is we middle-class white surburbanites, with all our things and tensions, who have a hard time letting go.

We even have a black friend in Africa who states that "where there is death, there is hope," because every tyrant and every dictator finally meets his death—the Khomeinis and the white racists and the Adolph Hitlers. Death has a way of finally getting rid of problems. And more than that—we now, thank goodness, are beginning to see that there are good deaths as well as bad, deaths accomplished in dignity and peacefulness and quiet acceptance.

And yet, for all our latest scientific and cultural advances in understanding death, we nevertheless know we daily fight against that unrelenting foe. We spend millions every year for face creams and hair dyes to mask the wrinkles and gray hairs, those signs that you and I are moving steadily toward death. We hide the dying down sterile corridors, behind the closed doors of hospitals, or we let them waste away alone in the beds of nursing homes. We hook them up to life-support machines and keep them artificially breathing. We transplant organs, hearts and kidneys, to gain just a little more time. And always we think that perhaps if we're just a little more clever, if we can just spend enough for heart research and cancer cure and miracle medicine, death can finally be cheated out of its final victory over us. But in the meantime, the things we fear most are the pain, the loneliness, the uncertainty of dying, and not knowing whether we can handle it. And then comes the chilling realization that handle it we must. Yes, certainly, the last enemy to be destroyed is death.

So how do you and I meet that final foe? How do we prepare ourselves for the death of loved ones and friends? And how do we prepare to meet our own certain end? The existentialist philosophers—Sartre and Pascal, Camus and Heidegger—tell us that we are never really free until we come to terms with the fact that we must die. So how do you and I come to terms with that fact?

Our expectation at this point in the sermon, of course, is that we will hear some words about the resurrection of Christ. And having been reassured once again that death is not really real, we can all go home to Sunday dinner in confidence and faith.

But that's not the way it works, is it? Words alone won't do it. In our New Testament lesson from Luke, Mary Magdalene and the other women went running from the empty tomb, and told the disciples that Jesus was risen. But, says Luke, "These words seemed to the disciples an idle tale, and they did not believe them." Words alone won't do it. In fact, simply the intellectual acceptance of the doctrine of the resurrection can be one more way we try to hide from the grim fact of death. And when the night falls and the dark comes, an intellectual faith is a very feeble light to see by.

Nor can science reassure us very much. In the last few years, we have all been flocking to read and to hear the accounts of those who have been revived from clinical death. Many of us have read the books by Dr. Elisabeth Kübler-Ross, or Raymond Moody's best seller, *Life After Life.* And it does give a person a certain comfort to hear the revived tell about the peace and joy and light they experienced before they were brought back to life. I myself like to think that perhaps my own dead parents experienced such happiness when they breathed their last. And yet, the truth that nags at the fringes of thought is that none of the people reported on in such studies ever really died. They all lived to tell of their experiences of being clinically dead. There is a mysterious boundary to death across which our doctors and scientists cannot step.

And so, good Christians, you and I have to look to one who has really died. We have to look to some pioneer of our faith who has gone into the wilderness of the grave before us. We have to look to one who has been there, to one who tasted the fruits of total extinction. And everywhere, the gospel stories and our creeds emphasize the reality of Jesus' end. "He breathed his last," says Luke. His blood and water flowed out, says John, from the spear thrust in his side. He descended into hell, the place of the dead, we affirm in the

Apostles' Creed. His lifeless body was laid in a cold rock cave-tomb and the door was sealed with a stone. Jesus Christ passed into the valley of the shadow of death before us.

How, then, do we know he is risen? What makes us think this one who was really and truly dead nevertheless has been raised up by God to new and eternal life? Well, the disciples in Luke did not believe the resurrection, until Jesus himself walked the road to Emmaus with them, and suddenly appeared in their midst in that upper room. And so it is too, with us. We know that Jesus Christ is risen because he now lives and rules in the midst of us.

You see, the assured witness to the resurrection is no intellectually accepted dogma. It is the glad cry of those who experience a living fellowship with a present Savior. It is the joyful shout of those who can say, "I know that my Redeemer liveth"—know it, know it to the depths of my being because he is here alive with me. Could anyone have convinced the apostle Paul that Jesus Christ was still dead? No, Paul said, it is not I who live, but Christ who liveth in me—the Redeemer by whose sacrifice my old life has been totally forgiven and done away—the present Son of God by whom I am strengthened to endure hardship and suffering and want—the glorified Lord for the sake of whom I forget all that lies behind and press on to hear his upward call to eternal life and glory.

Through every age, in every clime, from hut and hamlet and city, the church has been born and sustained and guided by one principal fact: Jesus Christ lives in the midst of its people and forgives and transforms and guides their lives. And out of that living fellowship with our Lord, we have joined our voices with Paul's, to say in the unshakable certainty of experienced faith, "In fact Christ has been raised from the dead."

The risen Christ is present right here and now in the midst of this congregation, and if in repentance and prayer and self-surrender we open our lives to receive his presence, we, too, shall know with absolute certainty that death has no final hold on us. O Christ,

I am continually with thee;
　　thou dost hold my right hand.
Thou dost guide me with thy counsel,
　　and afterward thou wilt receive me to glory.
Whom have I in heaven but thee?
　　And there is nothing upon earth that I desire besides thee.
My flesh and my heart may fail,
　　but thou art the strength of my heart
　　and my portion for ever.

(Psalm 73:23-26)

If in that faith, we open our hearts to the living Christ, who is present at this moment, the glad news told at the empty tomb will become good tidings for us also: "Why do you seek the living among the dead?" He is not dead. He is risen.

That is the certainty by which we can deal with the final foe, good Christians. And so why do you seek your lost loved ones among the dead? If they died in Christ, they are not dead, but alive in him, and you need not grieve as one who has no hope of ever seeing them again. No, oh no, picture them alive! See it in your mind's eye! See them vitally alive, joyful there in the company of the Lord you know so well. Christ has given your departed dear ones that abundant eternity of his that is the fulfillment of every good. And you shall meet and love and rejoice in that goodness, together once again. Because Jesus Christ has conquered the final enemy.

Why do you seek the living among the dead? Why do you despair of our world at times, and think that death has come up into our windows, or lies like a pall across a landscape pocked with evil and violence and hatred? Why do you hesitate to bring children into such a world, or imagine that there is no good purpose for living? This is Christ's world. He rules over it. He holds it in his lordly hand. He who has risen from the grave has won the battle with the powers of death and evil. And he shall establish his kingdom on earth even as it is in heaven. So trust that promise, trust his working. Join love and action to his. Work for good because you know the kingdom of good is coming. For Jesus Christ is its first fruit, and the death in our world will be replaced by his life.

Why do you seek the living among the dead? Why do you tremble at the thought of your own death, or think that God could not possibly receive you? Why do you think your life is too humble or stained—or perhaps better, too proud and rich—ever to be treasured eternally by a righteous and just moral God? It was precisely for your sinful sake and mine that God sent his Son to be buried in that tomb, and then to rise triumphant over every mean or immoral act that we have ever done. God in his mercy, his incredible mercy, has willed that we have life, good Christians—abundant life in Jesus Christ our Lord, And nothing, nothing can separate us from that Love who now stands here, risen, in our very midst. Not if we will trust him as our Lord over all our living and dying.

How do we meet the final foe? How do we deal with death? God in Christ has already dealt with the enemy for us. God in Christ has already won the decisive victory over the grave. "In fact Christ has been raised from the dead." I know, I know that our Redeemer liveth—yours and mine! Because he is here in our midst, at this very moment.

Amen.

G. Preaching for Pentecost

Pentecost is the season of the church, the long period between Eastertide and Advent in the liturgical calendar, when preaching is given over to exploring what it means to live as members of Christ's body, bearing his name, "Christian." The events that have been celebrated from Advent through Eastertide have created the church: because of the life and death and resurrection of Jesus Christ, the church has come into being and has been sustained and guided by God through the centuries. Now Pentecost sets forth what it means to be members of God's new covenant people in Christ.

The two sermons that follow deal with two different aspects of the Christian life: the first with Christian obedience and discipline, the second with the necessity for a persistent faith in the midst of perplexities and ambiguities. Both of them try to take a realistic attitude toward Christian living and to avoid that easy idealism and futile moralism that are unfortunately characteristic of so much preaching in our time.

The first sermon, "The Easy Yoke," was originally preached in St. John's United Church of Christ in Richmond. It was developed by employing a hermeneutical device that will always stand a preacher in good stead: that of taking a prominent figure of speech in the Bible and of following its meaning throughout the Scriptures. In this case, I was working with the figure of the "yoke," but there are hundreds of other such suggestive figures to be found throughout the Bible (see my *Creative Preaching*). The sermon was formed by investigating, with the help of a concordance, the meaning of "yoke" in Old and New Testaments. I pondered all of the passages containing the word, as well as their contexts. I then chose two of the passages, from Old and New Tetaments, and exegeted them as the focus of the sermon. These two Scripture lessons thus became the controlling guides, and the sermon was developed entirely out of their meanings.

When one writes a sermon on the basis of the Scriptures, however, one always finds that the Scriptures have brought one into the realm of Christian doctrine, and that is the case with this sermon too. My texts led me to a discussion of the relation of law and gospel. The sermon steadfastly proclaims the biblical, Reformed doctrine that we are enabled only by the Spirit of God in Christ to do what God demands of us. But when I developed this sermon, I did not set out primarily to expound that doctrine. I set out, first of all, to expound the meaning of the biblical texts. When finished, I nevertheless found that I had also dealt with one of the central doctrines of the Christian faith. The experience serves as a good example of the intimate relation of Bible and church theology.

This sermon deals with an aspect of Christian living that is, sadly, all too often neglected in our time—the necessity of Christian discipline. We live in a society and an age in which individual freedom has been elevated to the status of an inalienable right. Therefore, the fact that discipline, obedience—wearing a "yoke"—are necessities of the Christian life has become almost incomprehensible to our people. This message tries to correct that misunderstanding and thus brings the Scripture and Christian doctrine to bear on the errant views of our time.

As is true of the other sermons in this section, this message also tries to motivate the congregation to accept Christ's gracious invitation to wear his yoke. Our need for our Lord's "rest" is expounded at the beginning of the sermon; the joy and purpose and comfort given by wearing the yoke are described in the final portion. At the conclusion, on the basis of all that has gone before, Christ's invitation is issued once again.

Sample Sermon:

THE EASY YOKE

Scripture: Jeremiah 2:20-28
Matthew 11:28-30

"Come unto me, all ye that labor and are heavy laden, and I will given you rest" (KJV). This gentle invitation from a compassionate Jesus very often seems to us to sum up and to contain in capsule form the heart of the Christian good news—the warm assurance that we can cast all our burdens and problems and weariness on Jesus, and there find healing and solace for our troubled souls. It is like that invitation that we read so often outside church buildings—Enter, Rest, Pray—the invitation to leave behind us all the noise and complexity of our urban lives and to find a haven of peace and solitude. Handel set the words of this invitation to music in his oratorio, *The Messiah,* and it is the loveliest aria in the whole work. "Come," it seems to say, "cast yourself upon Jesus, and there find rest in a world of unrest."

Goodness knows, we need that invitation. No matter how well off we may find ourselves to be, we all have problems, anxieties, tensions, and perplexities from which we wish we could find relief. Just think of the difficulties you have with those who are closest to you. It seems to be a fact in this sinful world that we have our greatest worries in connection with those we love, precisely of course because they are the ones who touch our lives most deeply. We quarrel with them, or we disapprove of something they do, or we find ourselves at odds over some question. And even when all our relations are harmonious, we worry about what the future holds for those most dear. How good it would be to find peace and release from all our problems with loved ones!

How good too it would be if we could be delivered from our worries about ourselves. Most of us are just ordinary people, living rather ordinary lives, and yet common to all of us is a constant struggle to maintain a fingerhold on our own little niche in this world. We don't want to be wealthy or famous or great necessarily, but wouldn't it be nice if those around us just considered us important?—important enough to single us out for a "good morning," or important enough to value the work we do, or important enough to write us a letter, or to spend some time with us, or to call us on the phone? Every day of our lives we struggle to be the kind of persons or to do the kinds of things that will make us matter to someone else. And on those days when we feel discouraged and unimportant and no one seems to care, we very much need a haven of rest and love and comfort for our souls.

Add to that our search for security in this inflationary world and our occasional pondering over the purpose of our lives—especially as our years mount up toward their end—and it becomes clear why the words of our text speak so immediately to our hearts. In a world such as ours—given the nature of human life—we all labor and are heavy laden, and when Jesus promises us rest from our labors and relief from our burdens, we hear his words gladly.

The difficulty with this promise of Jesus' is, however, that it is attached to a condition. Jesus does indeed promise us rest for our weary or troubled souls, but he does so only on the condition that we are willing to accept another burden. He does so only when we agree to take his yoke upon us. "Come unto me, all ye that labor and are heavy laden . . . Take my yoke upon you, and learn from me." Such is the paradox of this gentle invitation: that we who are weary can be refreshed only by an additional responsibility—that we who are burdened down can have our load lightened only by carrying another added weight. That's enough to take all the joy out of this text and to make us groan with fatigue, unless we understand exactly what our Lord is saying to us here.

Jesus is in fact bringing us good news with his words—he always brings us good news—but he is telling us that good life for which we so long and labor, that life of peace and security and meaning and love, can be had only when we submit ourselves to his direction and place ourselves under his command. The figure is very clear: we are to wear a yoke—that crossbar which was laid across the shoulders of a draft animal and which had an encircling piece that went around the animal's neck. It was designed to keep the animal in line so he could pull a plow for a farmer. Jesus is the farmer, the master, you see, telling us when and how to go. And only as we submit ourselves to his command and rein can our life be full and whole.

We place great value on freedom these days. We seem to feel that we will solve the problems of our lives and world only if we can give freedom to individuals. We must have freedom to grow, freedom to learn, freedom from our repressions, freedom from society's restraints. The popular song title sums it up very well—just let me be "free to be me"; then everything will be fine and I can live a life full of joy and even gusto.

But the Bible takes the diametrically opposite view. The good life, it says, is never identical with unbridled freedom. It is never to be found in just "doing our own thing." Indeed, the Bible tells us over and over again that every time we reach for freedom and self-sufficiency, we fall into slavery.

There is that story about the prodigal son who, like most of us, wanted to be on his own. He cut himself off from his father and went out to that far country. And the freedom he sought to run his own life led him to a pigsty, and to hunger—a hunger that gnawed not only in his stomach, but also in his heart. Or there is that marvelous story about Adam and Eve in the garden, who decided they could be their own gods and shape their own futures. And so they grasped for the fruit that would let them live life on their own—the next scene shows them bickering and at odds with one another, as is so often true between husband and wife, in so many of our homes.

In fact, if we listened carefully to our Old Testament lesson for the morning, we heard the prophet Jeremiah tell us that when we try to be absolutely free, we become slaves to our beastly instincts. He was addressing seventh century B.C. Israel. "Long ago you broke your yoke and burst your bonds," he told her, and that could be a message addressed to each one of us. So what have we become by breaking the yoke of God and trying to go it alone? The picture the prophet gives is not a pretty one:

> Look at your way in the valley;
>   know what you have done—
> a restive young camel interlacing her tracks,
>   a wild ass used to the wilderness,
> in her heat sniffing the wind!
>   Who can restrain her lust?

The picture is of a beast in heat—driven by desire—captive to lust and instinctive drives to satisfy that lust. No, it is not a pretty picture, and it leads us to ask if, in our ill-gotten freedom, we could possibly fall so low. But I wonder if somehow it does not accurately picture the captivity of you and me—driven by all sorts of desires and fads and status-symbols that this world says are important. Tell me, friend, what are you driven to achieve or to get in twentieth century America? Or what is it social custom has persuaded you that you simply must be, if you're going to have worth and status and respect in the eyes of your neighbors? I don't think we need to kid ourselves—we too are driven, and far from being free individuals, we are slaves to this world's demands. And you and I do sometimes become quite beastly creatures toward one another as we run after the things and positions and powers that are held so temptingly before us. We look down on someone who has not achieved the status that we have. Or we trample over the feelings and rights of someone weaker than we are. Or we ignore or hate the one who has not adopted our superior views. And that's not only true in our society at large, but even in our homes, and even among those with whom we share the closest ties and bonds. We become beasts toward one another, and much, much less than the loving human beings our Creator intended us to be.

Our Scripture lessons tell us there is only one way we can become whole and free again, and that is by taking upon us that yoke that God in his Son invites us each to wear, the yoke of submission to God's commands and direction of our lives.

In his hilarious autobiography, entitled *In One Era and Out the Other*, Sam Levenson tells us about his bar mitzvah, his Jewish initiation at the age of twelve into all the rights and privileges of manhood. It is the time when a Jewish boy takes upon himself responsibility for fulfilling the Torah, for living according to the commandments of God. And in Jewish parlance, this has long been known as taking upon oneself the "yoke of the kingdom." This is what Levenson says of the experience:

(On my Bar Mitzvah), I came into my ethical inheritance. I was presented with the rights of manhood . . . I had to accept these rights in a speech written not by me, not by my elders, but by tradition: . . . "I now have the right to do right, to do justice, to do good, to serve humanity, to help the needy, to heal the sick, to look after my country, to strive for peace, to seek after truth, to liberate all mankind from bondage . . ." As I read, . . . I realized that I had . . . fallen into a moral trap. What rights? These rights were really obligations, commitments, responsibilities. I began to catch on. My rights and obligations (were) inseparable. . . . What tradition was telling me was that responsibilities exercised by all guaranteed the rights of all.[27]

So it is similarly with the yoke of Christ. If we would have the good life, if we would find rest and release from the burdens and problems of our life, then we must take on an additional load, the responsibility of doing Christ's will in the world—of following his commands.

But there is more than that to our Scripture lesson, and if we do not hear the rest, you and I will go away from this church feeling that an added burden has been imposed upon all the burdens that we already bear. But there is more! By the grace of God there is more! Levenson says that at the end of his speech, he was pelted with little bags of candy, a custom whose symbolism is quite clear: his manhood was going to be full of responsibilities—but they could be sweet. And that's the way it is with the yoke of Christ. It can be sweet. "My yoke is easy, and my burden is light," our Lord assures us. It is not something that adds to the load we carry, but rather lightens the load and makes it easy.

The prophet Hosea has a poignant portrayal of God in the eleventh chapter of his writing. He, too, uses this figure of God the farmer and of Israel wearing God's yoke. But then he says, the halter God put upon Israel to lead her along was a rope of love, and God bent down to feed her, as a farmer feeds his ox, and God was the one who lifted up the yoke from Israel's shoulders and helped her carry it.

God in Jesus Christ helps us carry his yoke, and so it is indeed an easy yoke and its weight is very light. Our Lord gives us commands to obey in this life, and he expects us to follow them. That is the yoke he lays upon us, the bridle upon our wanton self-rule and attempts to direct our own lives. But if it is only a command that Jesus gives us, then the gospel is not good news but law, and we are placed under a crushing burden of obligation that we cannot possibly fulfill. But Jesus does more than that. He not only gives us his commands to follow; he also gives us the power to obey them. He not only places a yoke upon us; he also helps us carry it.

You see, you and I are not very loving persons toward those around us, and yet we are placed under that command, that yoke, to "love one another as I have loved you." And beyond that, there is the order even to love our enemies. Judging by my own experience, I have the sneaking suspicion that every one of you has a difficult time fulfilling that command. Sometimes we have trouble just loving our families, much less our enemies. But Christ helps us—he carries the yoke for us; he floods our hearts with his Spirit of love and gives us the power to care, so that we love other persons in spite of ourselves and find that we can be compassionate. And then we realize with Paul, in our acts of mercy toward our neighbors and friends, that it is not we who live, but Christ who lives in us, giving us the power to be merciful.

Or there is that command, "Do not be anxious about your life, what you shall eat or what you shall drink, nor about your body, what you shall put on." These days, that's a hard word to hear, because prices are mounting, and we're watching our budgets, and we do indeed become anxious. That command is a bridle on our ways that contradicts all our natural reactions in American sociey—our natural reactions to scramble after every buck we can get, in the effort to secure our material welfare. But can you believe that Christ's presence with you brings an assurance about what the future holds, and gives an anxious breadwinner an inner peace which the world cannot give? Listen again to Paul: "I have learned, in whatever state I am, to be content. I know how to be abased, and I know how to abound; in any and all circumstances I have learned the secret of facing plenty and hunger, abundance and want. I can do all things in him who strengthens me." Yes, Christ helps us carry the yoke, and so it is an easy burden.

There is another reason why the yoke is easy. Christ's yoke is easy and his burden is light, because it frees us from futility. If you're wearing a yoke and pulling a plow, you're accomplishing something. You're not like that restless beast of a camel in our Old Testament lesson, going around in circles. You're doing a job for one who is getting ready to plant and harvest and bring in a crop. And that's exactly what is happening in this furrowed world of ours. God is plowing, pulling up the weeds of evil and getting rid of the rocks of rebellion, planting the seeds of his future garden, and preparing for his harvest, when the earth shall blossom forth with the fruits of righteousness and peace and joy. And by wearing his yoke and following his commands, we are participating in that task, and doing a work that we know will have solid and worthwhile results.

It's strange what sometimes happens to human beings along about middle age, for that's the time when we are most subject to feelings of futility. Our youthful energy and enthusiasms are gone, and with them our adolescent dreams. We begin to realize in the middle years that we will never do all those things and be all those persons that we imagined we would be when we were young. Death begins to catch up with our older relatives and acquaintances, and we suddenly realize that life is very, very short and that we ourselves no longer have time to conquer our own private universes. About this age, our children are grown and are starting to have their own problems, and we see that they may repeat many of the mistakes that we made. We get the empty feeling sometimes that maybe we really haven't made much out of life, and some of us have terrible regrets. Some even try to recapture their youth by entering into new love affairs or by masking wrinkles with cosmetics. It doesn't work, of course, because you can't turn back the years. And how many persons could be delivered from tragedy if they only realized that there is but one way to have a life full of meaning and purpose and accomplishment—by wearing that yoke, by participating in God's work, by joining in his plowing and planting and preparation of his garden on earth. In that work, there is indeed a sense of worthwhile achievement, and that makes the yoke of Christ very, very easy.

And then there's the joy! Just think of the joy of living under the direction of God! Somehow bearing Christ's yoke puts one in harmony with the life at the center of the universe, and that abundant life that Christ promised us becomes a present reality. Loved ones become new treasures of worth, valued despite all their flaws, because we live in forgiveness of one another, and in acceptance and caring. The world becomes a wonderful gift, given each day anew, by a Creator who not only knows how to splash the colors of a sunset across the sky, but who also faithfully arrays the flowers in our garden in a glory exceeding Solomon's. Our lives burst their little enclosed meanings and take on ultimate significance, and despite all our wrongs and past mistakes, we know ourselves nevertheless borne and carried in the everlasting arms. Even in the midst of the shadows of suffering and death, we find ourselves accompanied by one who never fails or forsakes us, though we descend to the depths of hell. Bearing the yoke of Christ brings with it joy—the joy of life in fellowship with God, who is the source of all joy and goodness, and contentment and peace.

A few years ago, I sat in a church in Oklahoma before the casket of my mother. As all of you know, who have found yourselves in a similar situation, there was great pain involved—the pain of loss, of grief, of separation from one held dear. But as those great waves of pain washed over me and the tears flowed freely, something else penetrated my consciousness—the words that were being spoken by the minister: "I am the way, the truth, and the life . . ." "I am the resurrection and the life . . ." "Come unto me all ye that labor and are heavy laden, and I will give you rest. Take my yoke upon you, and learn of me; for I am gentle and lowly in heart, and you will find rest for your souls." As those words made themselves felt in my heavy heart, I suddenly found myself lifted, borne up, reassured, comforted, strengthened. It was as if someone else were carrying my burden for me. The tears dried, and I realized that I was being led—led into a realm where there was joy, even at a funeral—led by one who held the future in his loving hands, who had conquered death and in whose care everything would turn out all right. It was that yoke, you see—Christ's easy yoke laid upon me, by which he was gently guiding me into his realm of life. And as I experienced the promptings of his love and his compassionate claim upon me, I thought to myself, "My Lord and my God! How can I refuse you?"

Christ wants to lay his yoke upon you, to guide you into joy and abundant life. When the invitation is so loving and the yoke is so easy, how can you refuse him?

Amen.

H. Preaching for Pentecost (continued)

This second sermon for the season of Pentecost was originally written for a Wednesday summer morning congregation at Chautauqua Institution, New York. I had the privilege of serving as chaplain for the week in that community and preached this sermon in the open-air amphitheater.

The sermon grew out of two desires on my part: first, to preach from this famous text in Genesis 32:13ff., and second, to deal with the day-by-day wrestling that is necessary to anyone who tries to live the Christian life in our society or in any society.

Certainly the Genesis text is one of the most important and profound to be found in the Old Testament. It encapsules the experience of Israel with her God, through her long history as his covenant people, and in doing so, it not only climaxes the cycle of Jacob stories but also sums up, in narrative form, what it means to be God's chosen people. Here, in a few vivid verses, is the story of our life as God's church. The text is, therefore, highly appropriate to the season of Pentecost, and every preacher should try to preach from it.

The wrestling that is portrayed in this text gives the lie to all of our homiletical temptations to portray the life of faith as one of clear-cut decisions, easy exercises of morality, and unalloyed joy untempered by suffering. We preachers sometimes portray the Christian life in those terms, but that portrayal is so unlike the actual experiences of the faithful in our congregations that they may conclude that we either know nothing about the Christian life or are afraid to picture it as it actually is for fear that no one will accept it. A faith that has a cross for its primary symbol cannot be characterized as promising only sweetness and light to its adherents. That cross speaks of blood and death, of evil and the powers of darkness—and our testimonies to the Christian life must take account of the actualities of that cross if they are to be believable.

Viewed from the standpoint of form criticism, the Old Testament lesson from Genesis 32 is a cult saga, which has been adapted to its contextual history of promise concerning Jacob, the patriarchs, and Israel as a whole. The original purpose of saga in the Old Testament was to draw its hearers (and later, its readers) into it and to allow them to identify with the story.

Precisely that purpose also informs this sermon and determines its form and content. In relation to every part of the story, the congregation is asked to identify with it. The sermon begins by briefly setting the stage and telling what is happening to Jacob. The congregation then is immediately asked to identify with Jacob's situation. After that, our story is made parallel to Jacob's: as Jacob wrestles with God, so we wrestle; as God has a purpose in wrestling with him, so God has the same purpose in wrestling with us; as Jacob's experience is unpleasant, so too ours can be; as the battle costs Jacob, so too it costs us. However, just as Jacob receives new life and good from his encounter, so may we, for it is finally the persistence of faith in the struggle that brings the blessing.

None of this parallelism between Jacob and us is set forth rigidly, in one-two-three lock step: that would be exceedingly boring. Illustrations, experiences, and attempts to engage the thoughts and emotions of the congregation, are woven into the whole. Nevertheless, it is the hermeneutical device of finding an analogy to the Christian life in Jacob's struggle that guides the course of this sermon from beginning to end. And that most often is the way the Old Testament narratives come alive for our people: when they see that Israel's story is their story because they are, in fact, the new Israel of God in Jesus Christ.[28]

Sample Sermon:

THE WRESTLING

Scripture: Genesis 32:13-32
2 Corinthians 4:5-12

If we read the Bible carefully, it becomes quite clear that the Scriptures present a strange new world to us—a world that we never see midst the hustle and humdrum of our daily round. But surely there is no story more strange in this strangest of books than the story that we heard for our Old Testament lesson. Jacob wrestles with a mysterious figure in the dark of night by the ford of the River Jabbok.

Jacob is on his way home, in the story, returning to Palestine after fourteen years spent in Mesopotamia with his Uncle Laban. And he is returning home, pretty much the same man that he was when he left in the first place. Jacob is a cheat. He is well-named, because that is what *Jacob* means: "cheat." Jacob's whole life has been spent in living up to that title. He cheated his brother Esau out of his birthright and blessing, out of his inheritance as the first-born, and when Esau therefore threatened to kill him, Jacob turned tail and fled to Laban's house. He spent his fourteen years with Laban, systematically cheating him out of his flocks and herds, and as Jacob appears in our Old Testament lesson, he is a very rich man. Probably the only decent thing he ever did in his whole life was to love Rachel with all his heart. But now he is on his way home again— even cheaters grow homesick. And the thought that is uppermost in his mind is that he must once again meet Esau. What will Esau do to him, after these fourteen years of absence? Will he let bygones be bygones or will he still try to kill him?

The news that Esau is coming to meet him, with four hundred men, is not reassuring to Jacob. However, crafty schemer that he is, Jacob sends ahead a huge present of goats and camels for Esau. He divides his caravan into two companies in the hope that at least one of them will escape. Finally, he sends his wives and children across the difficult

135

ford of the river in the dark of night. And then Jacob, the cheat, the schemer, the rich man, is left alone at the very rear, with only his own thoughts and fears to keep him company through the long hours of darkness.

I think we can probably identify with the scene that must have followed: the long night of tossing and turning on the cot, wondering what the morrow will bring, the anxiety about how it will all turn out, and the regret that we got ourselves into such a fix in the first place—the self-justifications and rationalizations for our own shoddy actions, the hatreds and angers turned over slowly in the mind, the planning of what we will say. We may not think of ourselves as cheats, but we have all shared Jacob's sleepless night, of restless fear and anxiety, and remorse and schemes for the morrow. He is very much like us there in the dark of the night, beside the ford of the River Jabbok, trying to plot one more successful strategy out of his own ingenuity and cleverness.

The clinker in the story, however, is that Jacob is not alone. A strange presence engages him in combat and wrestles with him till dawn. And Jacob becomes convinced that he is wrestling with God. In a similar picture from the Book of Job:

> A word was brought to me stealthily,
>   my ear received the whisper of it.
> Amid thoughts from visions of the night,
>   when deep sleep falls on men,
> dread came upon me, and trembling,
>   which made all my bones shake.
> A spirit glided past my face;
>   the hair of my flesh stood up.
> It stood still,
>   but I could not discern its appearance.
> A form was before my eyes . . . .

A form appears before Jacob's eyes, and fights with him in the darkness.

Do we not also share that experience of suddenly having to wrestle with some mysterious presence? We do not always know his name, anymore than Jacob did, but midst our schemes and hatreds and anxieties and long, restless nights and days, you and I, too, are haunted by some divine figure that engages us in combat.

What do you want to call it? Conscience—the voice within that goads and prompts and points out "This is the right!" when we so very much would like to take our ease and settle for the wrong? That might be an accurate title, except you and I are so easily able to win the battle with our own guilty consciences: Jacob, for all his conniving ways, never gave them a second thought. No, I think the Presence that haunts our days is much more than that. Francis Thompson called him the Hound of Heaven that pursued him down the corridors of the universe, with "noisèd feet" and "deliberate speed" and "majestic instancy." But maybe the title we really should give him is that of constant love—a love that engages us and wrestles with us and will not let us go.

It is a divine love that attacks you and me, and fights us for our souls, and keeps us restlessly tossing and yearning until we rest in him. We saw that divine love in the figure of a young man hanging on a cross on a hill called Golgotha, and now, try as we will, we cannot be rid of the presence of that man.

The scientist, Loren Eiseley, told the story of a troubled period of his life, when he was taking a cab from an airport into a large eastern city. He had to ride through the back streets of a slum area of the city, past an overgrown cemetery, an oil refinery, some crumbling houses, and finally, a neighborhood church. It was obviously a poor church, of an unknown sect—one of those gospel missions so typical of our inner city slums. In front of the church was a plain wooden sign, with these words written on it: Christ Died To Save Mankind. Is It Nothing To You, All Ye That Pass By? Eiseley writes: "I had seen fanatical sectarian signs of ignorant and contentious sects painted on rocks all over America . . . I had gazed unmoved on them all . . . But that plain white board . . . would not remove itself from my eyes . . . There was no evading it. 'Is it nothing to you?' I was being asked—I who passed by, who had indeed already passed, and would again ignore, much more sophisticated approaches to religion . . . Before my mind's eye, like an ineradicable note, persisted the vision of that lost receding figure on the dreadful hill of Calvary . . ."[29]

Yes, that is the figure that now wrestles with us in the dark of our secular souls, and we shall not rest until we come to terms with the love of Jesus Christ.

God engages us in battle in Jesus Christ because he wants to make us new men and women, just as he fought with Jacob to make him a new and different man. Jacob was a scoundrel and schemer all his life long, but by the grace of God he also had to become Israel—the father of the twelve tribes of the chosen people, the bearer of God's promise of blessing, the progenitor of a new humanity that would live out God's purpose on this earth. And God wrestled with Jacob to give him that blessing and to lock him into his purpose. God circled Jacob with those great strong arms and claimed him for his will. "Your name shall no more be called Jacob," he said, "but Israel." Your name is no longer "cheat," but one over whom God rules.

So, too, God in Christ wrestles with us to rule over our lives, to pull us into the good purpose that he is working out on this earth. The older I get, the more convinced I become that there is very little that happens to us by chance. I am no fatalist, like the Muslims, and certainly no determinist, like those who believe in astrology: we sinful human beings, in our proud folly and failures, are quite responsible for much of the chaos in which we live. But have you also noticed that inescapable unseen presence often sends our lives spinning off in the most surprising directions, as if indeed we were being hurled by some great wrestler's arm?

It is not always a pleasant experience. God can grab us and fight us and jerk us all the way round, to walk a new path that we had not dreamed of taking. I have seen an auto wreck do that in a person's life. I have seen it happen through serious illness. The prophets of the Old Testament would even say that God wrestles with us in international affairs—causing kingdoms to fall or rise, destroying or building nations.

Maybe that's something like what Paul meant when he

138

talked about the creation groaning in travail as it waits for the revealing of the sons of God. Our world and our lives are subjected to stresses and strains and groanings and travail, as God fights with us in Christ, to shape us according to his will and to bring us into his purpose.

Yet, at other times, his touch can be so very gentle and tender: what happily married Christian is not often convinced that God has led him to his mate? Or what mother has not been guided and nourished by some divine love through the love of her little children? God in Christ chooses a thousand ways to engage in his struggle with us, and it is all for the purpose of shaping and guiding and directing our lives into his good ways for them.

But it costs us something to wrestle with God, to have him hammer away at us until we reflect his will and can be worthy vessels of his blessing. The Bible repeatedly puts it in the figure of a potter with a hunk of clay, who pounds and whirls the stuff of us on his wheel, and molds us in his fingers, until he gets a pot that can offer someone a cup of cold water in his name, or until he makes an earthen vessel into which he can pour the treasures of his gospel. It is not easy to get pounded by that divine potter into conformity with his love. It sometimes is not a pleasant battle that God engages us in. We get wounded in it. Our pride gets trampled, and our self-righteousness gets humbled, and our self-will gets wrested from us. And we find ourselves with a cross on our back and a whole world waiting for compassion.

Jacob found that out. He limped away from his wrestling match with God. And the truth is that in the struggle, we have to die a little. We have to die to ourselves to become participants in the purpose of God. "Not my will, but thy will be done, O God." Wrestling with God finally always takes the shape of a crucifixion of our own desires and wills. As Paul puts it, we carry in the body the death of Jesus, that his life may be manifested in us.

But even that is not the most strenuous part of the wrestling. The most strenuous part, as every faithful

139

Christian knows, is the constant strain and struggle to see clearly what it is our Lord would have us do.

In Union Seminary in Richmond, Virginia, where I work, I have the happy task of teaching young men and women how to preach. And one error against which the young preachers constantly have to be warned is that of making it very easy to know the will of God. They would like to make everything black and white, with no shades of gray in between: on this side, all the right actions—on that, all the evil ones; on this side, the will of God—on that, the ways of the devil. But that is not the way life is, is it? We face a dozen decisions every day in which the will of God is not clear. Tell me, just what is the right thing to do with the welfare mess, or with the world hunger crisis? What is the will of God for the energy program or for the environment?

Any parent who has raised a child knows there are no easy Christian answers. Should Johnny go to private school or fight the battle of public education? Should Suzy be disciplined enough to continue her piano lessons or should she be allowed to quit? How tight a rein do you keep on a teen-ager, and where should he go to college? Is Mary mature enough to get married now, and does a parent have a right to interfere with a decision? We all give answers to those questions because we have to, but I am not sure our answers always reflect the will of God. We wrestle. We wrestle daily with how to translate the love of God in Jesus Christ into concrete decisions and actions.

Sometimes it is a matter of total perplexity as to just what God is doing with us. I am sure Jacob must have felt that way as he fought there beside the River Jabbok. Why this mysterious attack in the dark? Why this battle and this wounding? Why me, and why should I go limping off into the dawn? How often those have been our questions too, in the assaults and battles of life. "Why me, Lord? Why do I suffer this pain in my body, or this anxiety in my soul? Why did this loved one have to die? Why has this burden come upon me? What do you want of me, Lord? For goodness' sake, answer me!" The Bible is full of questions like that—from the Psalmists and Job, and Paul with his thorn in the flesh, and Jesus in Gethsemane. Indeed, as Israel looked back on her life with God, she saw it all summed up in the figure of Jacob, wrestling with mystery there in the dark. And our struggle with God is also often a struggle in the darkness with unfathomable mystery.

And yet Jacob's wrestling did not end in darkness, but at dawn with a rising sun. And he testified, I have seen the God who wrestled with me, face to face, and yet my life is preserved. Our wrestling with God in mystery and darkness is not all we have to say of him either. For we know who it is with whom we struggle. We have seen the light of the knowledge of his glory in the face of Jesus Christ, and we know he will preserve our lives also. And so with Paul, we can be afflicted and perplexed and struck down, but we are never destroyed or despairing or crushed, because finally the God who wrestles with us in Jesus Christ also saves and heals and sustains.

We reach that assurance in the same way that Paul and Jacob reached it—by hanging on to the God with whom we wrestle and refusing to let him go until he pours out on us his sustaining power and his comfort in every perplexity. We do not have all the answers to life. We do not know what the morrow brings. We do not even know if we shall survive at a quarter past dawn tomorrow—any more than Jacob knew during his long night there beside the River Jabbok. But one thing Jacob knew—that he fought with the one person who could give him all life and good. And he hung on to God and cried out in his struggle, "I will not let you go until you bless me!"

It is finally the persistence of faith that wins the battle in the struggle with Jesus Christ. He attacks us and fights us—make no mistake about it—and we shall never escape his demanding love that engages us here in our darkness, as we work out our little schemes for the morrow beside the river called Time. He hammers us and hurls us and turns us about, to set us facing a new path that will parallel his purpose. Always we are wounded in the struggle. Very often his working with us is a mystery. Very often we do not even know his will. But one fact is certain—he alone is the one who can give us all life and good.

So cling to him! Hold him fast! Out of your darkness, cry out in faith, "I will not let you go, Jesus, until you bless me!" For that faith brings light—and life—and the glories of the risen Son.

Amen.

NOTES

1. See especially James A. Sanders, *God Has a Story Too: Sermons in Context* (Philadelphia: Fortress Press, 1979); cf. also Edmund A. Steimle, Morris J. Niedenthal, Charles L. Rice, *Preaching the Story* (Philadelphia: Fortress Press, 1980); Eugene Lowry, *The Homiletical Plot* (Atlanta: John Knox Press, 1980).

2. See Donald E. Gowan, *Reclaiming the Old Testament for the Christian Pulpit* (Atlanta: John Knox Press, 1980); D. Moody Smith, *Interpreting the Gospels for Preaching* (Philadelphia: Fortress Press, 1980); G. von Rad, *Biblical Interpretations in Preaching* (Nashville: Abingdon Press, 1977).

3. An example of this viewpoint is Douglas Stuart's volume, *Old Testament Exegesis: A Primer for Students and Pastors* (Philadelphia: Westminster Press, 1980).

4. C. H. Dodd, *The Apostolic Preaching and Its Developments: Three Lectures with An Appendix on Eschatology and History* (1936; reprint, New York: Harper & Row, 1964).

5. Even Wisdom theology finds its fulfillment in Christ, according to John 1.

6. G. E. Wright, *The Old Testament and Theology* (New York: Harper & Row, 1969), pp. 100-101.

7. Raymond Brown's work on the Johannine community has shown this quite clearly. Cf. "The Church of the Johannine Epistles" Sprunt Lectures, *The Sub-Apostolic Churches in the New Testament* (Richmond, Virginia: Union Theological Seminary, 1980, lecture 4; sound recording, Union Theological Seminary Library, 1980).

8. Elizabeth Achtemeier, *Creative Preaching* (Nashville: Abingdon Press, 1980).

9. John H. Leith, unpublished paper.

10. James Weldon Johnson, *God's Trombones* (1927; reprint, New York: Viking Press, 1963), p. 17.

11. Annie Dillard, *Pilgrim at Tinker Creek* (New York: Harper & Row, 1974; Bantam Books, 1975), pp. 147-8.

12. Dillard, p. 140.

13. Lewis Thomas, "The Music of *This* Sphere," in *The Lives of a Cell: Notes of a Biology Watcher* (New York: Viking Press, 1974), pp. 20-24.

14. Ibid., p. 24.

15. Ibid., p. 22.

16. T. S. Eliot, "The Hollow Men," in *Collected Poems: 1909-1962* (New York: Harcourt, Brace and Co., 1936), p. 105.

17. Christopher Fry, *A Sleep of Prisoners* (New York: Oxford University Press, 1951; New York: Dramatists Play Service, Inc., 1953), pp. 61-62. (Passages cited are placed in inverse order.)

18. "The Hazards and the Difficulties of the Christian Ministry," in *Justice and Mercy*, edited by Ursula M. Niebuhr (New York: Harper & Row, 1974), p. 131.

19. "The Blessed Virgin Compared to the Air We Breathe," in *The Poems of Gerard Manley Hopkins*, 4th ed., W. H. Gardner and N. H. MacKenzie, eds. (Oxford: Oxford University for the Society of Jesus, 1967).

20. T. S. Eliot, *The Cocktail Party* (New York: Harcourt, Brace and Co., 1950), p. 136-7.

21. John Osborne, *The Entertainer* (New York: Criterion Books, 1958), p. 179.

22. "The Lantern Out of Doors," in *The Poems of Gerard Manley Hopkins*, 4th ed.

23. Amos Wilder, "Electric Chimes or Rams' Horns," in *Grace Confounding* (Philadelphia: Fortress Press, 1972), p. 13.

24. Ibid.

25. "When I Survey the Wondrous Cross," third stanza.

26. John Denver, quoted in "The Sunshine Boy," *Newsweek*, 20 Dec. 1976, 59-68.

27. Sam Levenson, *In One Era and Out the Other* (New York: Simon & Schuster, 1973), p. 184.

28. For a full discussion of the analogy between Israel and church, Old Testament and New, see Elizabeth Achtemeier, *The Old Testament and the Proclamation of the Gospel* (Philadelphia: Westminster Press, 1973).

29. Loren Eiseley, "Man: The Lethal Factor," *The Key Reporter*, 28, No. 3:4.